Here's all the great literature in this grade level of *Celebrate Reading!*

"Mom, Mom, My Ears Are Growing!"

And Other Joys of the Real World

Bingo Brown, Gypsy Lover
from the novel by
Betsy Byars
✳ *School Library Journal*
Best Book
✳ ALA Notable Children's Book

The Cybil War
from the novel by
Betsy Byars
✳ ALA Notable Children's Book
✳ Children's Choice

Remarkable Children
from the book by
Dennis Brindell Fradin

And Still I Rise
from the collection by
Maya Angelou
✳ *School Library Journal*
Best Book

**How It Feels to Fight
for Your Life**
from the book by
Jill Krementz
✳ Outstanding Science
Trade Book
✳ Teachers' Choice

**Fast Sam, Cool Clyde,
and Stuff**
from the novel by
Walter Dean Myers
✳ Children's Choice

**The Summer of
the Falcon**
from the novel by
Jean Craighead George
✳ Newbery Medal Author

Featured Poet
Maya Angelou

Look Both Ways
Seeing the Other Side

Free to Fly

A User's Guide to the Imagination

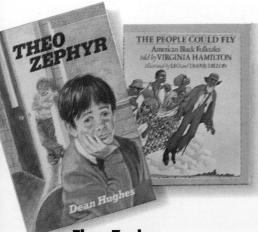

Theo Zephyr
from the novel by
Dean Hughes
❋ Children's Choice

The People Could Fly: American Black Folktales
from the collection by
Virginia Hamilton
Illustrations by Leo and
Diane Dillon
❋ *New York Times* Best Illustrated
❋ ALA Notable Children's Book

Joyful Noise: Poems for Two Voices
from the collection by
Paul Fleischman
❋ Newbery Medal

The Town Cat and Other Tales
from the collection by
Lloyd Alexander
❋ Newbery Medal Author
❋ American Book
  Award Author

The Foundling and Other Tales of Prydain
from the collection by
Lloyd Alexander
❋ *School Library Journal*
Best Book

Cinderella Finds Time
by Val R. Cheatham

In Search of Cinderella
by Shel Silverstein
❋ ALA Notable Children's Book

Glass Slipper
by Jane Yolen
❋ Kerlan Award Author

...And Then the Prince Knelt Down and Tried to Put the Glass Slipper on Cinderella's Foot
by Judith Viorst
❋ Christopher Award Author

Yeh Shen: A Cinderella Story from China
retold by Ai-Ling Louie
Illustrations by Ed Young
❋ ALA Notable Children's Book

Featured Poets
Paul Fleischman
Pat Mora
Shel Silverstein
Jane Yolen
Judith Viorst

Journey Home
and Other Routes to Belonging

Featured Poets
Gwendolyn Brooks
Edwin Muir

Arriving Before I Start

Passages Through Time

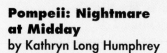

Just Like a Hero

Talk About Leadership

Featured Poet
John Greenleaf Whittier

Celebrate Reading!
Trade Book Library

Our Sixth-Grade Sugar Babies
by Eve Bunting
✸ *School Library Journal* Best Book

Goodbye, Chicken Little
by Betsy Byars
✸ Children's Choice
✸ Children's Editors' Choice
✸ Library of Congress Children's Book
✸ *New York Times* Notable Book

Dragon of the Lost Sea
by Laurence Yep
✸ ALA Notable Children's Book
✸ International Reading Association 100 Favorite Paperbacks of 1989

The Westing Game
by Ellen Raskin
✸ Newbery Medal
✸ Boston Globe-Horn Book Award

The Brocaded Slipper and Other Vietnamese Tales
by Lynette Vuong

The Jedera Adventure
by Lloyd Alexander
✸ Parents' Choice

The Endless Steppe: Growing Up in Siberia
by Esther Hautzig
✸ ALA Notable Children's Book
✸ Boston Globe-Horn Book Award Honor Book
✸ Lewis Carroll Shelf Award

Baseball in April and Other Stories
by Gary Soto
✸ ALA Notable Children's Book
✸ *Parenting* Reading-Magic Award

Tom's Midnight Garden
by Philippa Pearce
✸ Carnegie Medal Winner

The House of Dies Drear
by Virginia Hamilton
✸ ALA Notable Children's Book

Journey to Jo'burg: A South African Story
by Beverly Naidoo
✸ Notable Social Studies Trade Book

Jackie Joyner-Kersee
by Neil Cohen

Journey Home

and Other Routes to Belonging

TITLES IN THIS SET

About the Cover Artist
Teresa Fasolino lives and works in New York City, where she
specializes in oil painting. She has worked for advertising
agencies, book publishers, and major magazines (including
painting covers for *TV Guide* and *The New York Times
Magazine*).

ISBN: 0-673-82119-6

1995 printing
Copyright © 1993
Scott, Foresman and Company, Glenview, Illinois
All Rights Reserved.
Printed in the United States of America.

Acknowledgments appear on page 152.

  2345678910RRS9998979695

Journey
Home

and Other Routes to Belonging

ScottForesman

A Division of HarperCollinsPublishers

CONTENTS

SAVE ME A PLACE

YOSHIKO UCHIDA WRITES ABOUT "HOME"
AUTHOR STUDY
• • • • • • • • • • • • • •

THE PLACE I FIT IN
GENRE STUDY
• • • • • • • • • • • • • •

STUDENT RESOURCES
• • • • • • • • • • • • • •

Apple Is My Sign

by Mary Riskind

Mail Call

HARRY PICKED AT HIS PLATE of apple
fritters and scrapple. With the knot deep in his
stomach he just didn't feel hungry.

Up and down the table hands flew. Some boys
visited across the table, or side by side, and one
conversation leapfrogged over another. Harry followed
the discussion at the far end uninvited. A large-eared
boy wearing spectacles was telling a story about
someone signed 'Rapid Heart.' Harry wasn't certain,
but he thought 'Rapid Heart' was Mr. Thomas, their
proctor. His sign was the letter T tapped against the
chest, but Harry often noticed the boys using this
second sign.

Another fellow with dimples set deep into his
heavy cheeks ambled over to the table and joined the
conversation. The rest called him 'Mighty.'

Harry glumly stabbed a fritter. He didn't even understand their names. A few were obvious—like the boy with the wire-rim glasses. His name looked like two round circles over the eyes. Or the one beside him who went by 'Cowlick' for the yellow hair standing in a haystack above his forehead. But what about the boy who was signed by a tug on the right ear? Or 'Mighty'? And what about 'Rapid Heart'?

Spectacles pushed away from the table. He was hurrying the others to mail call. This was the moment Harry had dreaded all morning. He trailed behind the boys down the corridor from the dining hall to the high-ceilinged foyer and took a position outside the circle.

Their proctor, mustached, not yet crumpled by the day, appeared and lifted a mail pouch over their heads. The boys clawed like puppies.

On the opposite side of the foyer near the girls' stairs, a slender erect woman carried a second pouch. The girls bunched around her. Harry thought of his sisters. He missed Veve and Anna. Here—in the dining room, in study hall, in morning classes—the girls always were in another part of the room. Maybe it was like this in a hearing school. They never joined the boys' games and the boys never ventured up the girls' stairs. He wondered what they did there.

Mr. Thomas peered at a letter from the bag. His hands waved. Harry studied each gesture. 'B-r-o-w-n,' he announced, then finished with a snagging motion, as if pulling in a fish.

A boy in a blue flannel shirt stepped forward. He stuffed his envelope inside his cap without reading it. It was considered bad manners here to read mail under everyone's noses, but Harry saw them—during classes or over lunch—devouring their letters like stolen sweets. He hoped for a turn, too, for a letter saying

he could go home. He'd hoped for more than two weeks already.

Mr. Thomas turned the pouch upside-down and shook it. Empty again.

Harry bit his tongue to fight the brimming tears and ran out the front door of the school and down the steps. His foot missed the bottom step and he stumbled, almost falling.

When he reached the end of the driveway, he poked his head through the iron bars of the gate. Outside, a maple tossed her scarlet headdress and a golden-haired elm bowed. On the farm he loved the fall, when trees wakened from their green sleep and spoke to him in noisy orange and yellow tongues, as surely as if he could hear.

He turned from the trees and watched a horse-drawn trolley stop at the corner. Two people, a man and a woman, stepped down. He recognized the woman. She was the one who scowled whenever he went back for seconds on rolls or dessert. They disappeared around the corner in the direction of the back entrance.

He squeezed his eyes and squeezed the rails. If only the gate would swing free.

SOMEONE tugged his shoulder from behind, startling him. He didn't bother to see whose it was. He hit the hand away hard.

The hand was Mighty's. Up close he looked older than Harry's big brother Ray—maybe even twelve—and he stood at least a head taller. Harry glowered and braced himself for a shove. The boy stared, then handed over a small package. Harry's heart leapt. He recognized his father's handwriting.

The boy wheeled and headed up the walkway. 'Come,' he motioned. Harry lagged a few paces behind. But the slower he walked the slower the other boy walked. Finally the boy stopped and waited for him. His hands fluttered. 'New to school here?' he asked.

'Yes,' Harry answered.

'I here—soon four years,' the boy said. 'First not like. After-while you like. Work, work, but good fun, fooling, play tease. My name L_____.' He formed the letter L and rotated it over his stomach. 'Short for L-a-n-d-i-s,' he fingerspelled. 'What your name?'

'H-a-r-r-y.' Harry paused. 'I thought saw boys name you Mighty.'

'My second sign. Not necessary call me Mighty. I like L_____ better. You have sign?' Landis asked.

Harry flushed. 'Apple.' He hastened to explain. 'Older brother give-me name. Because while young always pick-up apples. Father has apple farm. Keep many, many apples in my pockets. Sometimes with worms. Not care. Love play, play with apples.'

'Good name,' said Landis. 'Home call me Baby. Once someone from school saw. Boys make fun. Make me very angry. We fight. I winner. Now name me Mighty.'

'Now understand.' Harry's fist circled his chest, then he extended his hand, palm out. 'Sorry push. Thank-you for bringing this.' Landis nodded.

They reached the school building. Mr. Thomas was waiting in the entranceway. 'Why skip-off?' he demanded.

Harry didn't answer. He pointed to his package.
'Let-me carry to sleep-room?'

'Yes. Go-on. Hurry.'

Harry cleared the wide wood stairs two at a time
and dashed for the row of neatly made beds nearest
the windows. Mrs. Slack glanced up from her folding
and sorting in the laundry adjoining the dormitory
room.

Mrs. Slack was like her pair of heavy black shoes,
sturdy and strict. The first week of school she had
rubbed a boy's mouth with soap for not paying
attention when she showed them how to make their
beds. Later that day Harry
had taken a small taste of
the yellow soap—the tiniest
bite—and knew he didn't
ever want her angry with
him.

'Why here?' Her face
furrowed as she mouthed
the hearing words and
signed at the same time.
Harry showed her the
package. She went back to
her work without asking
anything more. He breathed
a sigh of relief.

He reached under the
bed for his footlocker and
opened the lid so Mrs. Slack
wouldn't see. His hands

were trembling a little. He removed the string, carefully wound it, and put it in a pocket to save. He smoothed the brown wrapping and tucked it inside his locker. Then he spread the contents before him: two drawing pencils, a thin pocket knife on a fine chain, a soft charcoal eraser, a packet of new cream-colored paper, and a letter.

He turned the letter many times without opening it. Finally, he unfolded the page. The script was clear and flowing.

September 29, 1899

My dearest son Harry,

I enclose a small present from Mother and me. We hope these will help you feel happy at school. If you have time, Ray would like a drawing of school and of your friends.

We did not send you to Philadelphia because we think you are more trouble. I always dreamed of going to school. It is too late for me. Now I dream of schooling for you. You are better suited for school than Ray; and your sisters are too young. Ray does not love books. He will be a farmer like me.

In town there are only the hearing and their children. At Mr. Bertie's school you will meet people who are like us, you will learn a trade, and maybe some day you will help other deaf.

I know you are homesick. I talked again with Preacher Ervin, and he tells you to be patient. Soon you will make friends, have good times, and forget your troubles.

I think of you often and cross my fingers for you to be happy.

Your loving father,

Harry Berger

*H*ARRY CRUMPLED the letter. The hearing again. His father only wanted him away from the hearing. Didn't he know they were everywhere? Even at Mr. Bertie's?

He was so suspicious of them, expecting the shopkeepers in town to shortchange him, or blaming the friends Harry made there for anything he did wrong. Right up to the day he left for school, Harry had been teaching one of the boys from Muncy sign language—like Preacher Ervin—hoping that would change his father's mind. Freckles stood on the platform and fingerspelled 'G-o-o-d-b-y-e.' But Harry's father took no notice. Nothing could crack that granite stare, not when his mind was set.

Harry wadded the letter into a tight ball and threw it. He wanted to go home! He wanted to climb the apple trees. He wanted to bite into a sun-warmed apple and taste the burst of sweet wet. And he wanted to run—going and going until he dropped breathless.

He was tired of sitting at desks, standing in lines to brush his teeth, lines to get his food, and tired of grownups forever telling him to hurry.

The tears he'd held in check for days welled up and spilled over.

Something moved in the doorway. Landis. He waved. 'Come. Late. Mr. Thomas looking.'

Harry quickly wiped his face and stashed his presents under his pillow. Before Landis could ask questions, he ran past him to the boys' toilet room. 'T-T-T.'

Pictures

AFTER DINNER Harry unpacked a pair
of trousers and a couple of shirts from his locker and
hung them on the hooks above his bed—he guessed
he'd need them now that he was staying—and he
collected his charcoal pencils and paper to take with
him to study hour.

Landis took a seat across from him at the table and
nodded a greeting. Harry's head bobbed shyly.

He rolled the pencils between his fingers. They
were smooth, well-balanced, better than the ones he
usually had. His father must have been eager to please
him. He folded and unfolded the knife. He whittled
the end of one of the pencils to a fine point, and
played with the shavings until they crumbled and
scattered. Then he huddled over a sheet of the paper.

He rubbed the charcoal in short, even strokes. Soon the form of a building emerged, then out of that two long arms and a wide brick portico with stairs that swept around either side and met in front. A cobblestone walkway extended from the building through the trees to a high brick fence and iron gate. He penciled in the sign he remembered hanging in the front:

 THE BERTIE SCHOOL FOR THE DEAF

Landis reached over for his attention. 'Jealous,' he said. 'You draw very good.' He made his signs small to escape the study proctor's notice.

Harry felt his ears burn. 'For my brother. Never saw school.'

'Can you draw something for me?'

'Maybe. What?'

'Anything. Think idea yourself.'

Harry hesitated. 'Will try.' He started once, discarded the paper, started again and discarded that piece too. Suddenly he fell

to work. When he was finished he kicked Landis's foot, then passed his picture under the table.

Landis examined the drawing in his lap. His face broke into a smirk. Landis gave the picture to his neighbor on the right and fingerspelled 'H-a-r-r-y.' The boy looked over, winked his approval, and passed it to the person next to him, and so on, until the paper traveled full circle round the table.

All of a sudden the study proctor swooped beside Landis and ripped the drawing out of his hands. 'Whose? Yours?' All eyes in the long room turned.

Landis declined to say anything. The rest sat rigid.

The proctor spied Harry's pencils and the small sheaf of paper. 'Yours.' She pursed her lips as if she'd tasted something bitter, and stabbed a finger at the sketch. It was an outrageous caricature of Mr. Thomas with a great walrus mustache and heart-shaped head. 'Study. Not play.' She scooped up the drawing materials and returned with them to her desk.

Harry looked desperately to Landis.

'Not worry,' Landis said. 'Lady not cross.'

Harry was not persuaded. He was miserable.

Moments later Landis poked him. 'Watch-me,' he said with a toothy grin. He reached beneath the table. His hand reappeared blackened with boot polish. He rubbed his chubby left cheek, leaving a dark sooty mark. Harry watched, mystified.

Landis tapped Spectacles, who was sitting to his left, with his elbow. 'My face dirty?' he asked. Spectacles—one eye on Landis, one on the proctor—nodded his head yes and buried his nose in his book.

Then Landis tapped the person on his right side and repeated the question, pointing to his right cheek. 'No,' the boy on the right said.

'But he says my face dirty.' Landis pointed to Spectacles. The right-hand fellow inspected Landis's face again and shook his head no.

Landis turned to his left once more. 'Hey,' he nudged Spectacles, 'he says my face clean.' Landis looked right and left. 'Who right?' Hands on either side of Landis flared.

'Wrong!'

'You blind.'

'You stupid.'

'Who stupid? You stupid!'

Finally, Landis raised his hands as though to calm the unruly mob. 'Look.' He displayed first his left cheek to the boy on the right, then his right cheek to the left. Landis leaned back in his chair and rested his hands on his plump belly. He smiled from ear to ear.

'Wait.' Spectacles waved a warning toward the proctor, who was showing too much interest in their table. 'I will catch-you. You see,' he threatened.

'H-a, h-a, h-a,' Landis jeered.

The hour was finished. Landis and Harry walked together to the proctor's desk. 'New boy?' the proctor asked. 'Drawings very good.' She handed over Harry's art supplies but held back the pictures of Mr. Thomas and of the school. 'I keep pictures. Want show. What your name?'

'H-a-r-r-y B-e-r-g-e-r.' Harry's heart pounded. 'Pictures for brother.'

'Will give-back later.' She packed up her belongings, including the pictures. There was nothing for Harry to do but leave.

'Bad happen. Maybe make trouble for me because o-f pictures,' Harry said to Landis, as they walked to the dormitory.

'Nothing bad happen,' Landis said. 'Big heart, same father. That B-e-r-t-i-e's daughter. Better forget.' They proceeded a bit farther; then Landis stopped. 'You never tell-me. How-old you?' he asked. 'Me twelve.'

Harry smiled. He'd guessed right. 'Ten.'

'Ten? Short, whew. Think eight, eight. Maybe seven!'

'Short, all my family.'

'Good you have sign. Maybe boys hang name Short.'

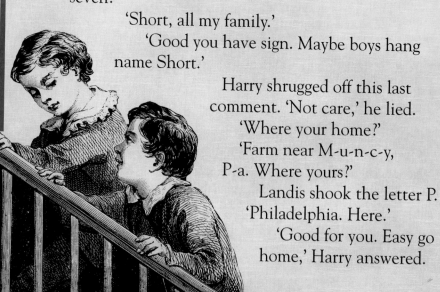

Harry shrugged off this last comment. 'Not care,' he lied.

'Where your home?'

'Farm near M-u-n-c-y, P-a. Where yours?'

Landis shook the letter P. 'Philadelphia. Here.'

'Good for you. Easy go home,' Harry answered.

'Maybe. Like school better. Home, only-one deaf. Small fun.'

'Your mother, father talking?'

'Yes.'

Harry was surprised. 'Both?' Sitting at the school dinner table he usually knew which children came from hearing families, especially the younger ones. Their hands were stilted, harder to understand. He liked this boy's signs. They were large and friendly. 'Brother, sister deaf?' Harry asked.

'No brother, sister.'

'Who teach-you sign-language?'

'Visiting preacher. Name E-r-v-i-n. During small.'

'I know preacher! I know, I know! Can hear? Yes. That same man who tell mother, father about deaf school.' Harry was elated that they might know the same person. 'Before, teach here. Now preach-around, around P-a farms. Bring news from all ears closed.' He extended the sign for 'all' to show how large the scope of Mr. Ervin's travels was.

'Yes, yes,' Landis nodded, 'same man.'

'Beautiful signs,' Harry said. 'My father not like hearing, but welcome E-r-v-i-n. I think because preacher sign good. Look same deaf.'

'E-r-v-i-n mother, father deaf.'

'Not-know before.' Harry's hands stopped. No wonder Preacher Ervin signed so comfortably. 'How you deaf?' he asked Landis.

'Sick. S-c-a-r-l-e-t f-e-v-e-r. Three years-old. Lose hearing. You?'

'Born deaf. Mother, father, all deaf.'

'Easy for you.'

Harry did not understand.

'You not lonely,' Landis explained. 'My mother,
father not like signing. First want me talk. Read-lips.'
Landis's face broke into a perfect imitation of the big,
chewing mouths the hearing people who worked
about the school used to make the children
understand.

Harry laughed and laughed. It felt so good to
laugh. Then he recalled his drawings. What if Mr.
Thomas saw them? 'Why Mr. Thomas signed Rapid
Heart?' he asked when the laughter slowed.

'You not know?' Landis's eyes widened and his
gestures grew excited. 'Mr. Thomas engaged B-e-r-t-i-e
daughter.'

'Lady who take my pictures?' Harry's hand went
to his mouth.

'Yes! That one.' Landis mimicked her stiff-necked
gait. 'Once boys find Mr. Thomas and daughter. Kiss,
kiss, kiss behind stairs. They think covered. He see
us—face red. Now we name-him Rapid Heart.'

Harry puckered his lips, made the sign of a wildly
beating heart, and swooned to the floor, rolling his
eyes heavenward.

'Yes. Yes. Perfect right,' Landis rejoiced. He
doubled over and tumbled onto the floor beside
Harry. The two boys lay there giggling.

Harry's sides were aching when they made their
way at last to the sleeping room. As they stepped
through the doorway, they saw Spectacles and several
of the other boys arrayed along the opposite wall.
A flurry of soft objects rushed toward them. It was

raining pillows, blankets, bathrobes, and towels.

Landis picked up a pillow and whacked the person nearest him over the head. 'Not me,' the boy protested. 'One watch.'

Harry grabbed a blanket and swung it in a whirlwind around his head.

They were pelted with more pillows. Landis and Harry ran from bed to bed, heaving back whatever they could lay their hands on, and from corner to corner searching for a defensible position.

They were standing on a bed when Harry ducked under a pillow and fell into Landis. The two of them collapsed, exhausted with fun. The other boys swarmed over them, tickling and roughhousing until Landis pleaded for mercy.

Spectacles stood over them. 'See?' he boasted, 'I told-you.'

After the gas lamps were turned down, Harry slipped out of bed and felt his way in the black night to Landis's bed. Harry fingerspelled, 'Y-o-u t-h-i-n-k B-e-r-t-i-e s-e-n-d m-e h-o-m-e f-o-r p-i-c-t-u-r-e-s.' He drew a question mark on Landis's palm.

Landis touched his hand. 'N-o. N-o.' His hands were big and comforting. Harry made his way back to bed and slept soundly.

Singer

FOR THE NEXT few days Harry made it a practice to bury himself in the thick of the lunchroom crowd or any line, and Landis delivered his mail. He hoped if Mr. Thomas didn't see him he'd forget to be angry about the picture.

In time he'd nearly forgotten the drawing himself, so it came as a rude jolt one afternoon when Mr. Thomas strode directly to him in the print shop. 'Come,' he motioned and led the way to the corridor. Harry's stomach fluttered.

'B-e-r-t-i-e want see-you,' Mr. Thomas said. The flutter turned to cold fear.

Mr. Thomas accompanied him to the headmaster's office, ushered him to the overstuffed chair opposite Mr. Bertie, then gazed out the window.

Mr. Bertie reached in a drawer and placed two sheets of paper on the desk blotter. There were his drawings. The bloated walrus-face lay on top. He stiffened.

'Drawing perfect,' Mr. Bertie flourished. 'You like draw?'

'Yes. Since little,' Harry signed weakly.

'Who teach-you?'

'Mother. And myself,' he answered, confused. These weren't the kinds of questions he expected.

'Want learn more?'

Now he was truly confused. He didn't know what to say. Mr. Bertie repeated his question. Hesitant, he nodded yes.

Mr. Bertie leaned over his desk. 'Wonder maybe you change. No-more printing. Go to t-a-i-l-o-r-i-n-g. Study clothing design. Study much more drawing. Cutting. Sewing. Think you like?'

Harry began to relax. What he'd learned in the print shop so far was tedious, though he enjoyed reading the finished copy.

'Well?' Mr. Bertie prodded.

He didn't know about tailoring, except his mother did do mending and sewing for townspeople in Muncy. On the other hand, he knew he loved drawing. 'Try?' Harry said.

The elderly man beamed. 'Fine. Settled. Mr. Thomas lead-you now.' He spoke a few words to Mr. Thomas, then he rose and handed over the sketch of the school to Harry. He held on to the other one. 'Allow-me keep this? Face very funny.'

Harry looked to Mr. Thomas, who had stopped before the coat-closet mirror. He was giving the tips of his mustache a satisfied twist. Mr. Bertie winked at Harry.

Harry grinned.

When Harry arrived at the textile room, he was surprised to see mostly girls—there were none in the print shop—and a handful of the older boys, who he knew slept in the third-floor dormitory. A few people paused from their work and smiled or gestured hello.

A short, quick man wearing a pincushion strapped to his wrist and a green visor showed him to a slant-top desk beside the windows. 'Since first day, you look, try new things. Tomorrow work. Any questions, ask—' He fingered the other pupils watching their exchange. 'I-f they not know, come see me.' And he was gone.

Harry hopped aboard the stool. The desk was arrayed with leads, pen points, holders, rulers, jars of ink, and other interesting items he didn't recognize. He reached first for a wood figurine. To his surprise it was flexible. The arms, the knees, the torso, bent. He twisted the form into a series of improbable positions—legs wrapped around the neck, crawling on all fours upside-down, or rolled into a ball.

A curly head grinned at him above the top of his board. The girl caught his eye. 'Silly,' he remarked, referring to the wood doll. 'What for?'

'Copy. Move any, how you want, then copy,' she said. 'Paper in drawer. Down right.'

In the drawer he found several kinds: heavy coarse sheets, satin smooth sheets, and thin translucent skins. He selected a pen point and holder and a piece of the heavy paper. After fumbling with the point, he finally jammed it into the cork handle. He was opening a jar of ink when the curly head peered over again.

'Shake first,' she said.

He shook. Black ink slopped out the sides and spattered on his fresh sheet of paper.

The girl laughed. 'No. No. Push-down-top first. Then shake. Better smooth paper for i-n-k. Rough good for black pencil,' she lectured.

Harry mopped up with a handkerchief. He was starting to feel irked with this know-it-all girl. He pointedly flipped the coarse paper clean side up and slid the edges under two thin slats hinged to the board. He wondered if she'd noticed he figured out how to hold the papers without her.

Then the pen dragged and ink oozed outward. The line he drew spread into a blotch. Phooey! The print shop was never like this.

The instructor stopped at Harry's table. 'Mistake.' He reached in the drawer and pulled out a smoother, harder sheet of paper. 'Best for i-n-k.' He whisked past.

Harry hunched down low, keeping his paper out of view of the curly-headed girl. He made a tiny mark with his pen. The ink behaved and stayed in its place. This was better. He unwound the figurine and molded it to resemble a person running; he sketched a front view first, then a side view.

'Good. Good. Perfect.' The instructor was at his side again. Harry sat a little straighter. The teacher gestured to the other side of his drawing board. 'A-g-n-e-s, show new boy sewing machine. And materials.' Agnes obediently climbed off her stool to stand next to him.

Agnes, Harry thought. His mother had an aunt named Agnes. He liked her pictures but he didn't like this Agnes.

Agnes stole a look at Harry's drawings. 'Nice,' she said. Harry scowled.

When Agnes led the way to the cutting tables, Harry loitered as far back as he could. The tables were heaped with fabrics. Agnes handed Harry several scraps. The material was soft, yet tightly woven and strong. It was finer than anything he had seen before.

'Man's coat, pants,' Agnes explained, 'for rich.' She extended the sign for 'rich' to suggest an awesome stack of money. It wasn't easy, but Harry managed not to smile.

Next she showed him to an empty machine. Ornate gold letters spelled out "Singer" across a black metal arm. Singer, he remarked to himself. Why Singer?

Agnes spun the wheel with her right hand. She pedaled the treadle and guided two pieces of material under the needle. 'Careful fingers. I-f needle in. Ouch.'

She halted a moment and reached for his hand. He pulled it away. She looked angry. 'Mule. Want show something.' He yielded reluctantly.

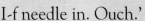

She placed his hand on the sewing machine, then resumed her stitching. The machine hummed into his fingertips with the light rumble of a satisfied cat under his hand. He smiled in spite of himself.

'Now me,' he begged. Agnes moved over on the bench.

The machine spun a couple of times, then stopped abruptly. 'What wrong?' he asked.

'Feet.' Agnes showed him how to keep his feet in rhythm with the wheel.

He made one or two false starts, but at last he had it. His feet rocked back and forth, back and forth, while the Singer purred. They took turns working the treadle the remainder of the afternoon and Harry listened with his fingers.

'Feel wonderful! Feel wonderful!' he said. 'Now I understand why named Sing e-r.' He repeated the sign for 'sing,' waving his arm as he'd seen the choir director do at Mr. Bertie's hearing church. Singer. It was the perfect name. Agnes wasn't bad either.

In a Deaf World

by Mary Riskind

I can hear, but I think of myself as a deaf person. Both of my parents were deaf, and I am deaf in much the same way that some children are first-generation Americans. Like many people who came to America from another country or culture or who grew up experiencing two cultures, I grew up in two worlds, the hearing world outside my home and the deaf world of my family.

In many ordinary ways my family was like any other family. My mother and father worked and drove the car. We had cats and a dog named Fifty. If I spilled food in the living room, I could count on a scolding, and my brother and sister and I argued a lot. The difference was that no one minded if we were noisy or slammed a door. We stomped on the floor to get my parents' attention, and in "deaf manners" it was okay to point. There was no telephone—my parents didn't need one (until I got into high school and wanted to talk to my friends).

Signing "Apple Is My Sign"

Even our pets seemed to know that this was a deaf family. Instead of barking, Fifty jumped in front of the kitchen window when he needed to be let in.

The biggest difference was that in my family we talked with our hands. My brother and sister and I learned to sign when we were babies, the same way most children learn to speak.

I was the oldest, so I was the interpreter. When my parents needed to talk to a hearing person, I talked for them—to the insurance agent, to the doctor, or to the clerk in the store. Once in a while I went to work with my father, who was a carpenter, to explain to him what a particular customer needed to have done. (If I wasn't around, my dad just wrote notes.)

Being the interpreter wasn't always easy. Sometimes I cheated a little. If what my parents wanted to say embarrassed me, I would change it, and if a hearing person said something I knew my parents would dislike or would not understand, I changed that too.

For me all of this seemed perfectly normal. Of course, I was aware that not everyone had deaf parents. All the kids who lived on our street or who went to my school had parents who could hear. But at the same time I knew several other families who were deaf like ours. There were social clubs for the deaf in our area, a church in town sponsored a signing minister who came once a month, and we visited each other's homes. This was our deaf community.

When deaf people get together, what they like to do most is talk. A good storyteller is always popular. That was my father. He loved to play practical jokes and he loved to tell stories about the tricks he played. My father was the kind of person who would wash smooth, round stones and leave them in the potato bag for my mother to "peel." Looking back, I realize now that many of his best stories poked fun at the deaf themselves. Deafness was never so seri-

ous that we weren't supposed to laugh.

Most people assume that sign language is the same as English. It is not. American Sign Language, often called ASL or Ameslan, is a separate language with its own vocabulary, its own grammar, and its own idioms or special expressions. I often describe sign language as sending a telegram. Only the important words are signed. Verb endings, plurals, and articles (a, an, and the) are omitted. Several English words may be condensed into a single sign.

In the chapters that you just read from the book *Apple Is My Sign*, the dialogue was written in telegraphic style much like sign language. You saw a mixture of both sign and fingerspelling. Fingerspelling is spelling out a word using the manual alphabet. Usually this is one of the first things people learn when they learn sign language. You also saw some phrases that were hyphenated, as in 'thank-you.' This was done to indicate that the signed equivalent is one continuous sign. One compromise I had to make in order not to confuse readers was to stick to English word order.

Not every English word has a sign. Generally, fingerspelling is used for words that have no signs, or sometimes to emphasize what is being said. Many times an English word is fingerspelled until a common sign evolves. The words *computer* and *video,* for instance, do not exist in my sign language dictionary, but I have seen the deaf in my area use signs that are adaptations of other signs. The sign they have created for *video* is similar to the sign for *movie*, but made with the *V* handshape.

Deaf people usually have unique sign-names that are given to them at home or at school. Harry's sign is "Apple" because he loved picking up the fallen apples on his father's farm. Sign-names are similar to nicknames. My father's sign was made by brushing the sign for "smile" back and forth at the right corner of his mouth. You can guess why.

Several of my dad's stories appear in the book *Apple Is My Sign*. My father had died before my son Paul was born, and when Paul started to express some curiosity about my father, I decided to write down some of his favorite stories for Paul. What began as a story for my son so that he could know something of my father in the end became a journey of self-discovery for me, a process of rediscovering the ways in which I, too, am deaf.

I'm proud to be a deaf person. It wasn't always that way. American Sign Language (ASL) is the fourth most widely used language in the United States today. But until recently the deaf were almost an invisible minority. I can still remember as a child being reminded by my mother to keep my signs low and out of sight, in order not to call attention to ourselves when we were in public.

Signing "Proud to be a deaf person"

My mother and I would not have that same conversation today. Attitudes toward the deaf by the hearing—and of the deaf toward themselves—are changing. ASL is also changing. At various times and places deaf children have been discouraged from signing. The point was to become as much like the hearing as possible in order to get along in a hearing world. The thrust in deaf education today is to use every available means for communication. Sign and speech are used simultaneously. As a result, more deaf children today learn Signed English, which supplies all the verb tenses, the little articles, and marker signs to spell out the context. For instance, in ASL "teach" can also refer to a teacher. In Signed English the sign for "person" is added to say "teach-person" whenever *teacher* is intended. Deaf children who grow up using Signed English will have a much easier time learning to read English.

There is also growing respect for ASL as a language. It is used increasingly in situations where spoken language is not practical—in underwater research, for instance, and to help mentally or emotionally disturbed people who cannot speak.

Another reason I wrote *Apple Is My Sign* is that many books about the deaf focus on the technology of being deaf, on hearing aids and body aids. It is such a limited picture of the world I knew. I hope you come away from Harry's story understanding that deaf people are far more than their physical disability, that deaf children have the same needs and the same aspirations that hearing children have.

Sometimes even I forget that. One day my mother and I were in the grocery store. She got very excited when she saw a newspaper headline about astronaut Sally Ride, the first American woman to go into space. I was proud, too, but my mother's pleasure seemed all out of proportion. 'Why so excited?' I asked. 'First woman. Next deaf,' she answered. New opportunities opening up for women meant to her that opportunities were opening up for the deaf as well.

I had to check my hearing prejudices and open my mind to the possibilities my mother saw. Why not? Why shouldn't the deaf pilot an airplane? Why shouldn't they pilot a spacecraft? In a deaf world it would be done differently is all—not better or worse, just differently.

Mary Riskind

Thinking About It

1. If you were Harry's parent, would you send him to a boarding school? Why or why not?

2. Harry's experiences at school are like a roller coaster: up when he hopes for a letter, down when one doesn't come, down when he is afraid of getting into trouble because of his drawings, and so on. Show "Apple Is My Sign" as a roller coaster ride and tell what the high and low points are.

3. Harry's sign was "Apple." Why? What is *your* sign? Why? What are the signs of three of your friends? Why?

ANOTHER BOOK BY MARY RISKIND

In *Follow That Mom!,* just when eleven-year-old Maxine wants to drop out of Girl Scouts, she finds out her troop has a new assistant leader—her mother! How can she get Mom to quit so that *she* can quit?

by Francisco Jiménez

THE CIRCUIT

from *Arizona Quarterly Magazine*

It was that time of year again. Ito, the strawberry sharecropper, did not smile. It was natural. The peak of the strawberry season was over and the last few days the workers, most of them braceros,[1] were not picking as many boxes as they had during the months of June and July.

[1] **braceros** (brä se′rōs), *contract farm laborers*

As the last days of August disappeared, so did the number of braceros. Sunday, only one—the best picker—came to work. I liked him. Sometimes we talked during our half-hour lunch break. That is how I found out he was from Jalisco,[2] the same state in Mexico my family was from. That Sunday was the last time I saw him.

When the sun had tired and sunk behind the mountains, Ito signaled us that it was time to go home. "Ya esora,"[3] he yelled in his broken Spanish. Those were the words I waited for twelve hours a day, every day, seven days a week, week after week. And the thought of not hearing them again saddened me.

As we drove home Papá did not say a word. With both hands on the wheel, he stared at the dirt road. My older brother, Roberto, was also silent. He leaned his head back and closed his eyes. Once in a while he cleared from his throat the dust that blew in from outside.

Yes, it was that time of year. When I opened the front door to the shack, I stopped. Everything we owned was neatly packed in cardboard boxes. Suddenly I felt even more the weight of hours, days, weeks, and

[2] **Jalisco** (hä lēs′kō), *a state in west-central Mexico*

[3] **Ya esora** (yä es ō′rä), *Ya es hora [It's time].*

months of work. I sat down on a box. The thought of having to move to Fresno and knowing what was in store for me there brought tears to my eyes.

That night I could not sleep. I lay in bed thinking about how much I hated this move.

A little before five o'clock in the morning, Papá woke everyone up. A few minutes later, the yelling and screaming of my little brothers and sisters, for whom the move was a great adventure, broke the silence of dawn. Shortly, the barking of the dogs accompanied them.

While we packed the breakfast dishes, Papá went outside to start the "Carcanchita."[4] That was the name Papá gave his old '38 black Plymouth. He bought it in a used-car lot in Santa Rosa in the winter of 1949. Papá was very proud of his little jalopy. He had a right to be proud of it. He spent a lot of time looking at other cars before buying this one. When he finally chose the "Carcanchita," he checked it thoroughly before driving it out of the car lot. He examined every inch of the car. He listened to the motor, tilting his head from side to side like a parrot, trying to detect any noises that spelled car trouble. After being

4 **Carcanchita** (kär kän chē′tä)

satisfied with the looks and sounds of the car, Papá then insisted on knowing who the original owner was. He never did find out from the car salesman, but he bought the car anyway. Papá figured the original owner must have been an important man because behind the rear seat of the car he found a blue necktie.

Papá parked the car out in front and left the motor running. "Listo,"[5] he yelled. Without saying a word, Roberto and I began to carry the boxes out to the car. Roberto carried the two big boxes and I carried the two smaller ones. Papá then threw the mattress on top of the car roof and tied it with ropes to the front and rear bumpers.

Everything was packed except Mamá's pot. It was an old, large, galvanized pot she had picked up at an army surplus store in Santa María the year I was born. The pot had many dents and nicks, and the more dents and nicks it acquired, the more Mamá liked it. "Mi olla,"[6] she used to say proudly.

I held the front door open as Mamá carefully carried out her pot by both handles, making sure not to spill the cooked beans. When she got to the car, Papá reached out to help her with it. Roberto opened

[5] **Listo** (lēs′to), *Ready; all set*
[6] **Mi olla** (mē ō′yä), *My pot*

the rear car door and Papá gently placed it on the floor behind the front seat. All of us then climbed in. Papá sighed, wiped the sweat off his forehead with his sleeve, and said wearily: "Es todo."[7]

As we drove away, I felt a lump in my throat. I turned around and looked at our little shack for the last time.

At sunset we drove into a labor camp near Fresno. Since Papá did not speak English, Mamá asked the camp foreman if he needed any more workers. "We don't need no more," said the foreman, scratching his head. "Check with Sullivan down the road. Can't miss him. He lives in a big white house with a fence around it."

When we got there, Mamá walked up to the house. She went through a white gate, past a row of rose bushes, up the stairs to the front door. She rang the doorbell. The porch light went on and a tall husky man came out. They exchanged a few words. After the man went in, Mamá clasped her hands and hurried back to the car. "We have work! Mr. Sullivan said we can stay there the whole season," she said, gasping and pointing to an old garage near the stables.

[7] **Es todo** (es tō′тно), *That's all*

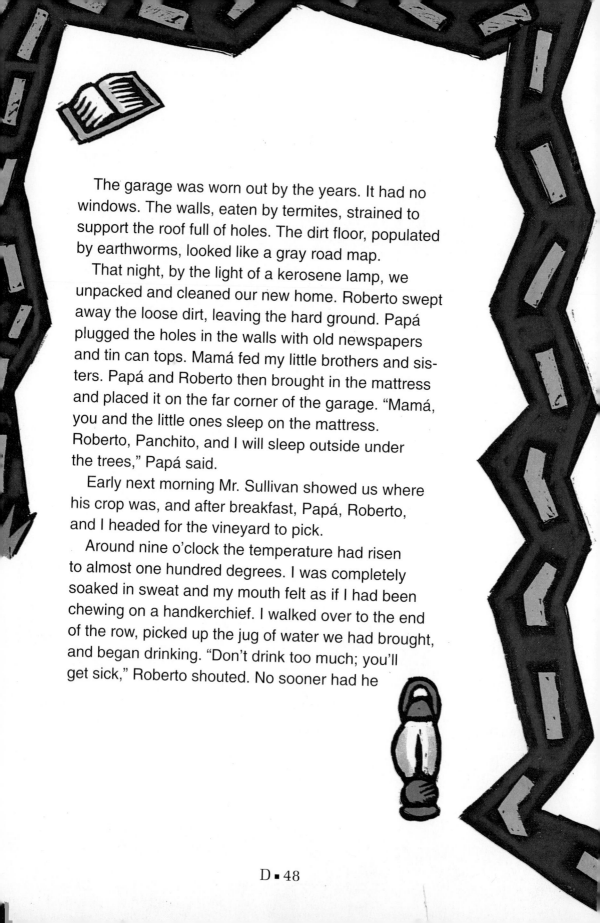

The garage was worn out by the years. It had no windows. The walls, eaten by termites, strained to support the roof full of holes. The dirt floor, populated by earthworms, looked like a gray road map.

That night, by the light of a kerosene lamp, we unpacked and cleaned our new home. Roberto swept away the loose dirt, leaving the hard ground. Papá plugged the holes in the walls with old newspapers and tin can tops. Mamá fed my little brothers and sisters. Papá and Roberto then brought in the mattress and placed it on the far corner of the garage. "Mamá, you and the little ones sleep on the mattress. Roberto, Panchito, and I will sleep outside under the trees," Papá said.

Early next morning Mr. Sullivan showed us where his crop was, and after breakfast, Papá, Roberto, and I headed for the vineyard to pick.

Around nine o'clock the temperature had risen to almost one hundred degrees. I was completely soaked in sweat and my mouth felt as if I had been chewing on a handkerchief. I walked over to the end of the row, picked up the jug of water we had brought, and began drinking. "Don't drink too much; you'll get sick," Roberto shouted. No sooner had he

said that than I felt sick to my stomach. I dropped to my knees and let the jug roll off my hands. I remained motionless with my eyes glued on the hot sandy ground. All I could hear was the drone of insects. Slowly I began to recover. I poured water over my face and neck and watched the dirty water run down my arms to the ground.

I still felt a little dizzy when we took a break to eat lunch. It was past two o'clock and we sat underneath a large walnut tree that was on the side of the road. While we ate, Papá jotted down the number of boxes we had picked. Roberto drew designs on the ground with a stick. Suddenly I noticed Papá's face turn pale as he looked down the road. "Here comes the school bus," he whispered loudly in alarm. Instinctively, Roberto and I ran and hid in the vineyards. We did not want to get in trouble for not going to school. The neatly dressed boys about my age got off. They carried books under their arms. After they crossed the street, the bus drove away. Roberto and I came out from hiding and joined Papá. "Tienen que tener cuidado,"[8] he warned us.

After lunch we went back to work. The sun kept beating down. The buzzing insects, the wet sweat,

[8] **Tienen que tener cuidado** (tyen′en ke te ner′kwē ᴛʜä′ᴛʜō), *You have to be careful*

and the hot dry dust made the afternoon seem to last forever. Finally the mountains around the valley reached out and swallowed the sun. Within an hour it was too dark to continue picking. The vines blanketed the grapes, making it difficult to see the bunches. "Vámonos,"[9] said Papá, signaling to us that it was time to quit work. Papá then took out a pencil and began to figure out how much we had earned our first day. He wrote down numbers, crossed some out, wrote down some more. "Quince,"[10] he murmured.

When we arrived home, we took a cold shower underneath a waterhose. We then sat down to eat dinner around some wooden crates that served as a table. Mamá had cooked a special meal for us. We had rice and tortillas with "carne con chile,"[11] my favorite dish.

The next morning I could hardly move. My body ached all over. I felt little control over my arms and legs. This feeling went on every morning for days until my muscles finally got used to the work.

It was Monday, the first week of November. The grape season was over and I could now go to school. I woke up early that morning and lay in bed, looking

9 **Vámonos** (bä′mō nōs), *Let's go.*

10 **Quince** (kēn′se), *Fifteen*

11 **carne con chile** (kär′ne kōn chē′le), *a dish made of meat, beans, and red peppers*

at the stars and savoring the thought of
not going to work and of starting sixth grade
for the first time that year. Since I could not sleep,
I decided to get up and join Papá and Roberto for
breakfast. I sat at the table across from Roberto, but
I kept my head down. I did not want to look up and
face him. I knew he was sad. He was not going to
school today. He was not going tomorrow, or next
week, or next month. He would not go until the cotton
season was over, and that was sometime in February.
I rubbed my hands together and watched the dry,
acid-stained skin fall to the floor in little rolls.

When Papá and Roberto left for work, I felt relief.
I walked to the top of a small grade next to the shack
and watched the "Carcanchita" disappear in the distance in a cloud of dust.

Two hours later, around eight o'clock, I stood by
the side of the road waiting for school bus number
twenty. When it arrived I climbed in. Everyone was
busy either talking or yelling. I sat in an empty seat
in the back.

When the bus stopped in front of the school, I felt
very nervous. I looked out the bus window and saw
boys and girls carrying books under their arms. I put

my hands in my pants pockets and walked to the principal's office. When I entered I heard a woman's voice say: "May I help you?" I was startled. I had not heard English for months. For a few seconds I remained speechless. I looked at the lady who waited for an answer. My first instinct was to answer her in Spanish, but I held back. Finally, after struggling for English words, I managed to tell her that I wanted to enroll in the sixth grade. After answering many questions, I was led to the classroom.

Mr. Lema, the sixth-grade teacher, greeted me and assigned me a desk. He then introduced me to the class. I was so nervous and scared at that moment when everyone's eyes were on me that I wished I were with Papá and Roberto picking cotton. After taking roll, Mr. Lema gave the class the assignment for the first hour. "The first thing we have to do this morning is finish reading the story we began yesterday," he said enthusiastically. He walked up to me, handed me an English book, and asked me to read. "We are on page 125," he said politely. When I heard this, I felt my blood pressure rush to my head; I felt dizzy. "Would you like to read?" he asked hesitantly. I opened the book to page 125. My mouth was dry.

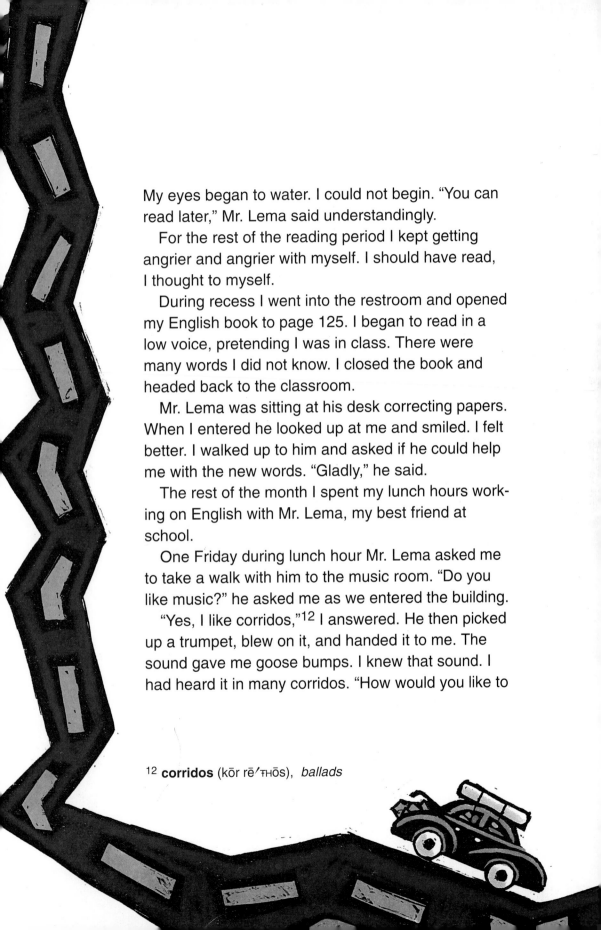

My eyes began to water. I could not begin. "You can read later," Mr. Lema said understandingly.

For the rest of the reading period I kept getting angrier and angrier with myself. I should have read, I thought to myself.

During recess I went into the restroom and opened my English book to page 125. I began to read in a low voice, pretending I was in class. There were many words I did not know. I closed the book and headed back to the classroom.

Mr. Lema was sitting at his desk correcting papers. When I entered he looked up at me and smiled. I felt better. I walked up to him and asked if he could help me with the new words. "Gladly," he said.

The rest of the month I spent my lunch hours working on English with Mr. Lema, my best friend at school.

One Friday during lunch hour Mr. Lema asked me to take a walk with him to the music room. "Do you like music?" he asked me as we entered the building.

"Yes, I like corridos,"[12] I answered. He then picked up a trumpet, blew on it, and handed it to me. The sound gave me goose bumps. I knew that sound. I had heard it in many corridos. "How would you like to

___

12 **corridos** (kōr rē′тнōs), *ballads*

learn how to play it?" he asked. He must have read my face because before I could answer, he added: "I'll teach you how to play it during our lunch hours."

That day I could hardly wait to get home to tell Papá and Mamá the great news. As I got off the bus, my little brothers and sisters ran up to meet me. They were yelling and screaming. I thought they were happy to see me, but when I opened the door to our shack, I saw that everything we owned was neatly packed in cardboard boxes.

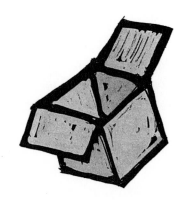

THINKING ABOUT IT

1. What did you hope for the narrator as the story went along? How did you feel after the last sentence of the story?

2. Did you expect the ending of the story? Did the narrator expect the ending? Did the author put clues into the story that it would end this way? Explain your answers.

3. If you could change the narrator's life so that the ending of the story could be different, how would you do it? What would be different?

Lyle

by Gwendolyn Brooks

Tree won't pack his bag and go.
Tree won't go away.
In his first and favorite home
Tree shall stay and stay.

Once I liked a little home.
Then I liked another.
I've waved Good-bye to seven homes.
And so have Pops and Mother.

But tree may stay, so stout and straight,
And never have to move,
As I, as Pops, as Mother,
From land he learned to love.

D▪59

Edwin Muir

The Way

Friend, I have lost the way.
The way leads on.
Is there another way?
The way is one.
I must retrace the track.
It's lost and gone.
Back, I must travel back!
None goes there, none.
Then I'll make here my place,
(The road runs on),
Stand still and set my face,
(The road leaps on),
Stay here, forever stay.
None stays here, none.
I cannot find the way.
The way leads on.
Oh places I have passed!
That journey's done.
And what will come at last?
The road leads on.

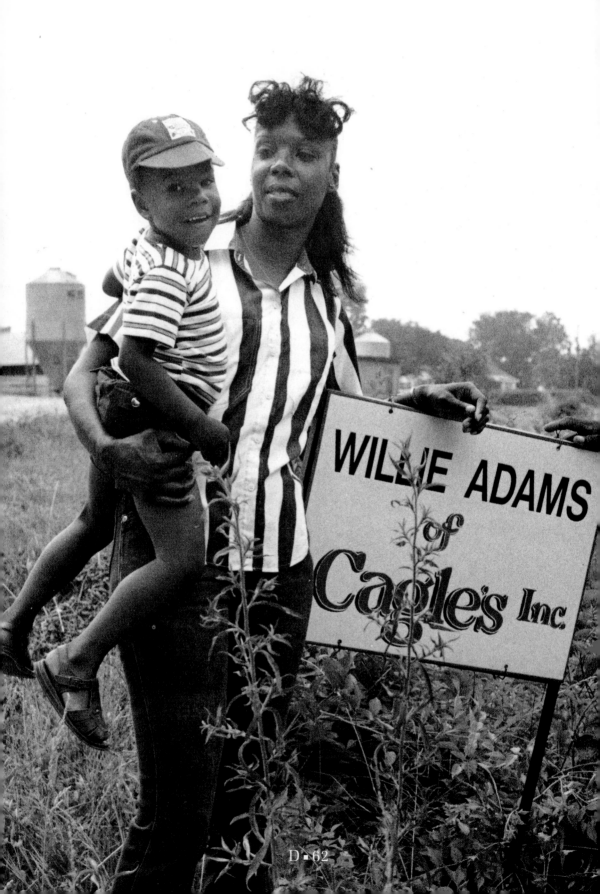

THE
ADAMSES
of Georgia

Photo Essay by
George Ancona

Text by
Joan Anderson

Willie Adams's house and farm in Greensboro, Georgia, are tucked away behind the towering pines that line the east Georgia highway.

"At the fork in the road, bear left," Willie says, "and go down the hill and over a bridge. You'll see our sign. The house is at the end of the road."

Willie lives with his wife, Linda, daughter, Shonda, son, Cedric, and his mother, Rosie.

"I spent my childhood following my grandfather as he steered the horse-drawn plow and worked these ninety-two acres," Willie says. "In those days, the fields around here were full of cotton, peanuts, and corn."

Despite hard times, Willie's grandfather did whatever was necessary to hold onto the land.

"Then, when I was just fifteen, he took ill and could no longer work," Willie remembers, "and things had to change if the farm was to survive."

"That's how I eventually got into chicken farming," he says. "There was no way I could manage growing crops and go to school at the same time. Besides, with synthetic fiber becoming more and more popular, cotton was on its way out. My mother and I were forced to change our way of farming altogether."

They phased out crops and began raising beef cattle, improving their pastureland to allow them to feed the new herd. Twelve years ago, Willie added two poultry houses to his farm. "In this business you always have to look ahead to what will sell. Poultry farming doesn't depend on weather, because the chickens are kept in specially built houses. As long as they are fed properly, you're pretty much guaranteed a healthy chicken at the end of eight weeks."

"We live a simple life—real quiet and peaceful," says Rosie, sitting on the porch with her grandchildren on her lap. "There's always a breeze on this front porch, because the house sits on a little knoll and catches the air.

It sure is a perfect place to raise children. Lets 'em see down-to-earth living. That way they learn how things are. Living on a farm allows you to go down to grass roots and know that something can always be created from the soil."

Every day, Cedric sets off for the fields with his red wagon.

"He collects whatever is growing out there," his grandmother says. "Willie did the same thing when he was little, and look what happened to him!"

Everyone has a place here. Linda Adams tends to the poultry houses when her husband is off in the fields. In the afternoon she says good-bye to the children and goes to work in a nearby sock factory.

"Most of the women out here work away from the farm at least part-time," she says. "It adds a steady income for us, along with what we get from the chickens. If farming is in your blood and you want to stay on the land, you do what needs to be done to make that possible."

Twice daily, Willie drives five miles in his pickup truck to a tract of U.S. Forest pastureland where his seventy Beefmaster cattle graze. "I rent the land for a small fee," he says. "It's one way the government is trying to help the small farmer."

"Here in Georgia the cattle can stay out all year long," Willie says as he unloads buckets of feed. "They're good animals. I wouldn't feel like a farmer if I didn't have a herd of cows."

"A few years back something very exciting happened to me," says Willie. "I began meeting other black farmers who seemed to love agriculture as much as I did. At the time, we were all struggling, working independently of each other. Most of our wives had jobs, and none of us could afford hired hands. Gradually it occurred to me that perhaps we could help

each other, that surely there would be strength in our combined ideas. And so I formed a cooperative in which the members would experience a sense of kinship, share knowledge and labor from time to time, and offer each other moral support—just like it would be if we were brothers working the same farm. The co-op is like an extended family farm."

Today ten members, all of whom share common roots, belong to the cooperative. They are Willie and Linda Adams, I. V. and Annie Henry, Leroy Cooper, Melvin Cunningham, Roger Lemar, Frank Smith, Robert Williams, and Mrs. E. M. Neal.

Descended from Africans brought as slaves to this country over one hundred years ago to till the white man's land, these fifth-generation farmers truly know the cycles of agriculture.

Thinking About It

1. Which of the photos in this selection would you be willing to be part of? What would you be doing or saying or asking?

2. The article tells you some advantages of belonging to a cooperative. What are they? What may be disadvantages?

3. Many famous artists have done "pastoral scene" paintings in which farm life is shown as calm and peaceful. Would the Adamses agree? What would you put into a painting of a modern farm scene?

Another Book About Farming

The Strength of the Hills, by Nancy Price Graff, beautifully describes a single day in the life of the Nelson family, the owners of a small dairy farm in Vermont.

Waka's Gift

from *A Jar of Dreams*
by Yoshiko Uchida

Being Japanese during the 1930s is hard for eleven-year-old Rinko Tsujimura. Her classmates tease her, and Wilbur Starr, a business rival of her father, continually threatens her family. Only Aunt Waka, visiting from Japan for the summer, can show Rinko that being Japanese is as important as being American. Now that Aunt Waka is returning to Japan, Rinko must fulfill her promise to wear the kimono Aunt Waka gave her when she arrived.

A promise is a promise, so on Sunday after dinner, I got out the kimono Aunt Waka had brought me. It was in my bureau drawer still folded nice and flat inside its soft rice paper wrapping.

One good thing about kimonos is that they don't wrinkle if you fold them properly on the seams. Also, almost anybody can wear the same size because there are no buttons or snaps. If you're short, you just pull up more to make a tuck and tie it in place with a silk cord. I thought that was pretty clever when Aunt Waka pointed it out to me.

She had to help me get dressed in the kimono because I certainly couldn't do it by myself. She made sure I overlapped the left side over the right (boys do the opposite), and she wound the wide brocade *obi* around and around my middle and tied an enormous knot in back.

J felt as if I was bound up in a silk cocoon and could hardly bend down to put the white *tabi* socks on my feet. It was hard to walk, too, with the thongs of the *zori* —the sandals—digging in between my toes, and I discovered why Aunt Waka took those small steps when she walked. You have to, with the long narrow kimono coming down to your ankles.

"There, you look beautiful," Aunt Waka said, when she'd finished. "Go look at yourself in the mirror."

I padded over in small steps to the bureau and looked at myself. I held out my arms to look at the white peonies blooming on the long blue silky sleeves. I turned around and twisted my head to look at the knot of the *obi* in back. I knew then exactly how Aunt Waka felt when we made her get into western clothes.

"That's not me," I said.

Aunt Waka smiled. "I know how you feel, but it's you all right."

Then she hurried me out to the parlor to show Mama and Papa how I looked.

Mama's eyes really lit up when she saw me. "Why, Rinko, you look so pretty." And then she said, "Stand up straight now." But she didn't say it the way she usually does in order to improve my posture. She said it as though she wanted me to feel proud of myself.

I guess Papa was about as pleased as Mama. He stood back and studied me as though he was taking a picture of me.

"I suppose you wouldn't consider going to the hospital to show Uncle Kanda* how you look, would you? That would really cheer him up, you know."

"Never in a million years," I said.

So Papa told Joji to get the box camera he got for Christmas and take my picture for Uncle Kanda. Aunt Waka got her camera too. We all trooped outside, and I stood beside the peach tree squinting at the sun.

"Stop squinting, Rinky Dink," Joji said.

*a good friend of the family, though not their real uncle

"Don't you call me that, Joji Tsujimura," I said. I raised my arm to give him a whack and that's when he took my picture.

"Smile," Aunt Waka said, focusing her camera.

I blinked, and that's when she squeezed the shutter.

Mama wanted a picture with all of us in it, so I went over to get Mrs. Sugar. She looked exactly the way I thought she would when she saw me wearing a kimono. Her mouth made a big **O,** but no sound came out.

Then she said, "Why, it's my sweet little Japanese Rinko," and she gave me a hug. But it was hard to hug her back being wrapped up like a package in all that stiff brocade.

Mrs. Sugar lined us up in front of Papa's garage and made sure she got his big sign in the picture too.

"There," she said when she'd taken three pictures. "This will be a fine commemoration of your aunt's visit."

She sounded just like the people at church. They are always taking pictures to commemorate Easter or Memorial Day or somebody's baptism or even somebody's funeral.

I could hardly wait to get out of the kimono when we were finished with all the picture-taking. Aunt Waka untied and unwound
everything, and I shook my bones loose to get my circulation
going again.

"Boy, am I glad to get out of that thing," I said.

Then I remembered the kimono was a present from Aunt Waka,
and I tried to think of something nicer to say.

"I'll have Mama put it in her trunk and cover it with mothballs,"
I said.

I guess that wasn't exactly what Aunt Waka wanted to hear
either. I thought she probably would've liked me to say I'd get it
out and wear it once in a while.

But she didn't say that. She just smiled and said, "Ah, Rinko,
you certainly are a child of America." Then she turned serious and
said, "But don't ever forget, a part of you will always be Japanese,
too, even if you never wear a kimono again."

"I know," I said. "It's the part that makes me feel different and
not as good as the others."

*I*t was the strangest thing. Suddenly, it was as if I'd opened a faucet in my head and everything inside came pouring out. I told Aunt Waka all about how I felt at school—how the boys called me names and the girls made me feel left out. And I told her a terrible secret I'd kept to myself and never told anybody, ever.

Once when there was going to be a PTA meeting at school and we had notes to bring home, I tore up my note and never gave it to Mama. I did it because I didn't want Mama to go. I didn't want her bowing to all my teachers and talking to them in the funny English she sometimes uses. I didn't want Mama to be ignored by everybody and left sitting in a corner. I guess maybe I was a little bit ashamed of Mama. But mostly I was ashamed of myself.

"I hate always being different and left out," I told Aunt Waka.

Aunt Waka was folding my kimono and *obi* on top of my bed, smoothing them out carefully so there would be no wrinkles. She wrapped them up again in the soft rice paper and tied them up just the way they were when she'd brought them. Then she put them aside and sat down on my bed.

"I think I understand how you feel, Rinko," she said in a soft whispery voice. "When I was young and couldn't run or play with my friends, they used to tease me and call me a cripple. They often made me cry."

I thought of the old photograph of Aunt Waka standing with the crutch. "But you were smiling anyway," I said, as if she'd know what I was remembering.

"Just because you're different from other people doesn't mean you're not as good or that you have to dislike yourself," she said.

She looked straight into my eyes, as if she could see all the things that were muddling around inside my brain.

"Rinko, don't ever be ashamed of who you are," she said. "Just be the best person you can. Believe in your own worth. And some-day I know you'll be able to feel proud of yourself, even the part of you that's different . . . the part that's Japanese."

I was still in my slip sitting next to Aunt Waka and wriggling my toes as I listened to her. And then it happened, like a light bulb had been switched on in my head. At that very minute I finally knew what made Aunt Waka seem so special. She was exactly the kind of person she was telling me to be. She believed in herself and she liked herself. But mostly, I guess she was proud of who she was.

I hate saying good-bye to somebody I like, especially when I don't know when I'll ever see that person again. I didn't even want to think about saying good-bye to Aunt Waka.

She tried to cheer me up. "Who knows, Rinko," she said. "Maybe someday you'll come to visit me in Japan."

"I could start a 'going to Japan' jar," I said.

"Yes, it could be your 'jar of dreams.' "

I knew I couldn't do it until after I'd filled up my "going to college" jar. Maybe not even until after I'd finished college and become a teacher.

But Aunt Waka clasped her hands together and talked as though I might be coming next year.

"Wouldn't that be wonderful, Rinko?" she said. "I'll be waiting for you."

Mama stuffed Aunt Waka's willow basket with all kinds of presents for Grandpa and Grandma. She packed boxes of chocolate kisses and cube sugar and tins of coffee and bags of walnuts and a big white tablecloth she'd crocheted. It was round and white and looked like a giant snowflake. She'd been working on it every night since before Aunt Waka came, and she finished it just in time for Aunt Waka to take home with her.

"What else can I send home with you?" Mama asked, looking around the house for something more. She probably would've put in a few dozen eggs and one of her sponge cakes if she could.

When the willow basket couldn't hold another thing, Papa tied it up and Aunt Waka packed away her small Buddhist altar and all her clothes. Then she spent the last two days saying good-bye to everybody.

J went with her to see Uncle Kanda. He'd gone home now and was doing fine and only needed one of the church ladies to come make supper for him. He was sitting in a wicker chair with a blanket wrapped around his knees, and he certainly looked a lot better than when I saw him in the hospital. He told Aunt Waka, "This is one of the nicest summers I've ever had."

"Even if you cracked your head?" I asked.

"Yes, even with that."

"Perhaps you will come to visit your native land someday," Aunt Waka said to him.

Uncle Kanda looked off into the distance, as if maybe he was seeing the green rice fields in his old village.

"Perhaps someday," he said. But he didn't sound like he really meant it, and Aunt Waka didn't say she'd be waiting.

I had a strange feeling they'd probably never see each other again. But I could tell by the way they smiled at each other that they'd always be friends.

Aunt Waka said good-bye to Tami and her mother at church. I guess Aunt Waka never did mind going to church with Mama every Sunday, even if it wasn't a Buddhist temple. She just said faith was faith, whether we got it in church or in a temple. And she even learned the words to "Onward, Christian Soldiers."

I guess Tami's mother was disappointed she hadn't been able to match Aunt Waka up with Uncle Kanda.

"You will be back one day, won't you?" she asked.

Aunt Waka said she certainly hoped so, and I guess Tami's mother thought she'd have another chance next time. But I knew better.

The night before Aunt Waka left, Mrs. Sugar invited us all to her house for dinner. It was the first time we all got invited together, and Mrs. Sugar used her best china and her plated silverware and baked a big ham.

She gave Aunt Waka a beaded coin purse and several hugs and said she might even go to Japan someday to visit her.

And Aunt Waka said, "I'll be waiting for you," just the way she said she'd wait for me.

The next morning, Mama, Papa, Joji, and I took Aunt Waka to San Francisco to the same pier where we'd gone to meet her. Another big ship was berthed there, waiting to take her back to Japan.

Mrs. Sugar would've been surprised at all the hugging Aunt Waka and Mama and I did when it was time to say good-bye. And crying, too, especially Mama.

When the ship was about to sail, the small band on the first-class deck played "Aloha Oe," and everybody threw pastel-colored streamers from the railing down to their friends on the pier. I was afraid the third-class passengers wouldn't get any, but, thank goodness, they did.

Aunt Waka threw her first roll of colored tape to me. I guess because it was my favorite color, blue. Then she threw one each to Mama and Papa and Joji, so we each had a streamer linking us to Aunt Waka up there on the ship.

There must've been hundreds of pink and yellow and lavender and blue streamers all tangled up and billowing in the breeze. It was all so beautiful and sad, what with the music and all, I wanted to cry.

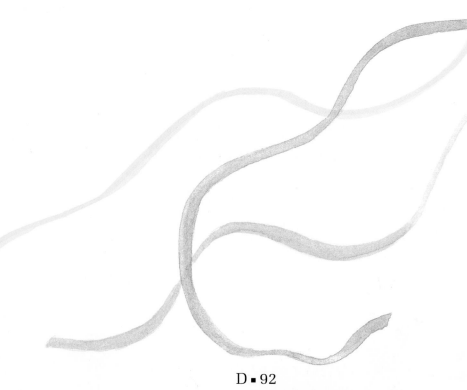

When the gangplanks were drawn up, the band played "Auld Lang Syne." Mama cried some more, and Papa held his streamer in one hand and waved his hat with the other.

"*Sayonara*, Waka . . . good-bye . . ." he was shouting.

"Take care of yourself," Mama called, but I don't think Aunt Waka heard her, because the ship's whistle gave three long blasts, and then it slowly began to pull away from the pier.

"Come on, Joji," I said, and we walked along the pier trying to keep up with the ship and make our streamers last as long as we could.

I could feel the roll of tape spinning on my finger, slowly at first and then faster and faster as the ship moved out to sea.

"So long, Aunt Waka. Come back!" Joji yelled.

He tried to wave, and his yellow streamer snapped and went flying off with the wind.

But I was still connected to Aunt Waka. She was like a kite flying way up in the sky, with only a thin piece of string to keep her linked up with me.

"I'll come see you in Japan!" I yelled as loud as I could.

Now that I couldn't talk to her, I thought of a million things I wanted to say to Aunt Waka. I wanted to tell her that this had been one of the best summers of my entire life, and that from then on I'd think of everything that happened to me as "Before Aunt Waka" or "After Aunt Waka," because *she* was the one who'd made the difference in our lives, not Wilbur Starr.

I guess Aunt Waka had stirred us up and changed us all so we'd never be quite the same again. I was really beginning to feel better

about myself—even the part of me that was Japanese—and I almost looked forward to going back to school to see if maybe things would be different.

But it was too late to tell her. Aunt Waka was gone. All I could do was just stand there straight and tall, hoping Aunt Waka could still see me with my hand stretched up high over my head.

I stood there a long time watching Aunt Waka's ship going further and further away from me, until finally my blue streamer was all unrolled and went flying off into the summer sky.

Thinking About It

1 As you read "Waka's Gift," what memories did you have of someone who influenced you? Did you, too, have to say good-bye? Tell about the experience.

2 Aunt Waka, how did you help Rinko feel better about being Japanese? What did you really think of Rinko?

3 Rinko's "jar of dreams," the jar in which she was saving money for the future, was a "going to college" jar; then Rinko was going to start a "going to Japan" jar. What would your "jar of dreams" be for?

Living with Strangers

from *Journey Home*

by Yoshiko Uchida

Yuki Sakane and her family have been released from Topaz, a concentration camp in Utah which housed West Coast Japanese Americans during World War II. While Yuki's family waits in Salt Lake City for clearance to return to California, Mr. Sakane must make monthly visits to the Immigration Board. The reports are an unpleasant ordeal for the man. Mr. Sakane has just returned from one such visit.

The wonderful smell of fried pork and onions was drifting through their apartment and down the steps to welcome him, but instead of remarking how good supper smelled, Papa slumped wearily into his big armchair.

"Wretched creature," he muttered.

"Who—me, Papa?"

"No, no, Yuki. Of course not you."

Mama came from the kitchen still holding her long cooking chopsticks. "How did it go today, Papa?" she asked.

"More of the same," Papa answered with a long sigh.

Then Yuki remembered. It was the day of the month Papa had to report to the parole officer at the Immigration Board. She still felt a stab of anger when she recalled how the three FBI men had taken Papa away like a common criminal. But he had been one of the lucky ones, released early to join them in Topaz. Now that he was out of camp, however, he had to report to a parole officer each month and would have to until the war ended.

"What'd he want to know today?" Yuki asked.

"He asked in which direction I would shoot if I had a gun and was standing between American and Japanese soldiers."

"*Mah!*" Mama was flabbergasted.

"So what'd you say, Papa?"

Papa took off his glasses and rubbed his eyes. The question was so ridiculous, he began now to smile at the thought of it.

"What could I say?" he asked with a shrug. "I told him I'd point the gun straight up and shoot at the sun."

"And then what'd he say?"

"He made me fill out the same fifteen-page questionnaire all over again."

No wonder Papa was in a bad mood. But his black moods never lasted long, and already his anger was melting away. "I suppose the poor fool only thought he was doing his job."

"Well, it's over until next month," Mama comforted. "Now come and enjoy your fried noodles. You'll feel better."

Papa got up and started toward the kitchen. But before he left the living room, Yuki saw him take the evening newspaper from his coat pocket and stuff it quickly into the wastepaper basket. That was strange because Papa never threw out a paper until it was at least a day old. Was there something in the paper that Papa didn't want them to see? Yuki intended to find out as soon as supper was over.

As soon as she could, Yuki retrieved Papa's newspaper from the wastepaper basket and took it to her room. She found the article about the 442nd RCT* and now she knew why Papa had hidden it from Mama.

The 442nd had been sent to France and was in a terrible, bloody battle in the forests of the Vosges Mountains trying to rescue a battalion cut off from water, food, and medical supplies. The words "withering enemy fire" kept echoing in her mind as Yuki read about the steep, rugged mountain forest dotted with mines, and the artillery shells exploding against the trees and showering the men with shrapnel.

Yuki felt weak in the knees just thinking of Ken in the midst of all that terror. And when she went to sleep that night, her nightmares shifted from the dust storms of Topaz to the battle in the Vosges Mountains.

It was raining and cold, and somehow Yuki was over there with Ken, struggling up a slippery mountain path, with a full pack on her back and an M-1 rifle in her hand. She could hear the German shells coming closer and closer as she slogged through miles of mud, watching closely not to step on a mine. Her bones ached, her eyes

*Yuki's older brother, Ken (Kenichi), is serving in the United States Army in France with the 442nd Regimental Combat Team (RCT).

burned from lack of sleep, and she could feel the cold rain seeping through her clothes, wet and damp against her skin.

She was trying hard to catch up with Ken, but he was "going for broke," giving everything he had, trying to prove he was a good American. And he wouldn't wait for her.

"Ken!" she shouted, but he never turned around, and soon he disappeared entirely into the mountain mists.

"Ken!" she called out a second desperate time. Then she woke up shivering.

What did soldiers do when it rained, Yuki wondered. How did they ever get their socks dry? Suppose all Ken had was a cold, muddy foxhole to jump into, with water puddling up all around, his boots and socks soaked through? Suppose Ken got killed before he could ever have a nice hot meal or sleep again in a warm, dry bed? Yuki couldn't bear even to think about it.

"Kenichi Sakane," she murmured. "You'd just better not get yourself killed over there, or I'll never ever forgive you."

The next evening Yuki broke Mama's best crystal bud vase. Mama had wrapped it up in her gray wool sweater and carried it with her all the way from Berkeley to Topaz in the desert, and finally to Salt Lake City. It was a special vase she used when she put a flower beside the photographs of Yuki's grandparents on the anniversary day of their death. It was the vase she used, too, for Hana, the older sister Yuki had never seen, who had died when she was only one year old and was buried in the cemetery in the hills of Oakland.

Mama never talked about Hana, but she always kept a snapshot of her on the bureau. It was turning brown now, but the silver frame it was in was always polished and shiny. It would have been nice, Yuki sometimes thought, to have a sister who'd always be there to do things with.

The day before they had to leave Berkeley and go to the concentration camp, Mama had gone to the cemetery to say good-bye to Hana. She took her a bouquet of all the flowers she could gather from their garden and told her not to worry. She told her Papa was in a prisoner-of-war camp and the rest of them were about to be sent to another kind of camp, but they'd all be back when the war was over, and for her to rest in peace until then. She had pulled out the weeds around the small gray tombstone and then watered one last time the flowering cherry tree she and Papa had planted there.

And now Yuki had broken Mama's crystal vase and she'd never have it again to put beside Hana's picture, or anybody else's. It had slipped through her soapy fingers just as she was putting it on the dish rack and crashed to the floor in a mass of sharp, jagged pieces.

Yuki felt so awful she wanted to cry. She usually didn't cry when she'd done something stupid. Sometimes she just tried to cover it up by acting as though it weren't important. Another time she might have swept up the pieces before Mama saw them and used her own money to buy her another bud vase.

But tonight it was different. She knew how much the vase meant to Mama, and she also had this terrible feeling that it was a bad omen. It meant something had happened to Ken. She just knew it. All day she'd had these anxious feelings about Ken and now she knew why. Something had happened to him, and maybe she'd never see him again.

"Oh, Mama," Yuki wailed.

Mama put her arms around her and held her close. "That's all right, Yuki," she said. "It was an accident."

And then as though she knew exactly what Yuki was thinking, she said, "Look at it this way, Yuki. Maybe my vase was broken in order to spare your brother. Maybe it was destroyed in place of something happening to Ken."

Mama smiled a sort of half-smile, as though she were remembering something from long ago.

"That's what your grandma would have said, Yuki. She used to say that objects sometimes have lives of their own and that sometimes they die in order to spare us."

Yuki knew Mama was trying to make her feel better. Mama swept up the broken pieces of glass and put them in a newspaper. She folded the newspaper neatly and carefully, almost as though it were a gift. Then she laid it gently in the garbage can, giving the vase a sort of burial rather than just dumping it out unceremoniously.

"There," she said, brushing her hands. "Now I think I'll write a letter to your brother."

Mama had already written him two letters that week, but they hadn't had a letter from Ken in over a month.

"No news is good news," Papa said.

But suppose Ken were wounded, Yuki thought, and his company had moved on without him. Suppose nobody found him and he was lying there in the rain, bleeding to death and . . .

Yuki felt a sharp sadness that surfaced into a sob.

She found one more piece of glass that Mama had missed and dropped it carefully into the trash can. She almost felt as though she'd killed Ken herself.

Christmas had seemed sad and empty this year because for the first time in her life Yuki didn't have any close friends to share it with.

Mama did her best to bring the Christmas spirit into their apartment. She bought a small crêche at the five-and-ten-cents store and put it up on the table in the living room.

Mary and Joseph and the baby Jesus were there, surrounded by the animals of the barnyard and the shepherds and the three wisemen with their gifts. It was beautiful and peaceful, as though Bethlehem were right there in their living room.

"Maybe the world has gone crazy," Mama said, "but the Christmas story is still the same. It's important to remember that, Yuki, and not forget what Christmas really means."

"Uh-huh."

Yuki understood. But she couldn't help wishing things were different.

"Don't keep wishing for what can't be," Papa told her. "Be happy for this special Christmas we have now."

But Yuki thought of the Christmases back home in Berkeley when the house was filled with the tantalizing smell of Mama's cookies baking in the oven and the glorious fresh green smell of the Christmas tree by the front window. This year

Mama was too busy to do all the things she used to do back home.

Yuki remembered the Christmas Eves when she delivered Mama's cookies to the neighbors, and Mrs. Jamieson would ask her to stay for a cup of sweet, creamy cocoa.

Then there was the Christmas program at their small Japanese church, all decorated with red and green paper streamers and bells, and a giant Christmas tree with enormous colored balls and silver tinsel. The church was always crowded on Christmas Eve when the Sunday School put on its program.

Yuki remembered how cold it was in the drafty parsonage parlor where they changed into their costumes for the nativity scene, squealing and shivering around the small gas heater as they shook off their heavy coats and new Christmas clothes. Yuki was usually one of the angels, dressed in scratchy white gauze with a silver halo that slithered down on her forehead. She giggled and whispered with her friends until it was time to appear on stage. But once she was in her place and the choir sang "O Holy Night," somehow the special feeling of Christmas wrapped her up like a comforting blanket on a cold, foggy night.

Afterwards, Mama and Papa's friends gathered around, telling her in their soft Japanese voices how beautiful the program had been. Maybe that was part of it, Yuki thought now. She missed her own friends, but she missed Mama and Papa's friends, too, with their Japanese talk and their genial bows and even the smelly yellow pickles they brought to picnics. Maybe that's what was wrong with this Christmas. Here in Salt Lake City their world was made up only of *hakujin*— white people who were strangers to them in a strange city that wasn't home.

The doorbell suddenly jangled Yuki out of her dreams. Papa was at work and Mama had ventured out, though it was snowing hard, bundled up in her warmest coat and scarf, to buy groceries. "We have to eat," she'd said, "snow-storm or not."

Yuki ran down the steps, saw a shadowy person on the other side of the lace-covered glass of the front door, and wondered who it could be. When she opened the door, she saw it was a boy with a telegram, and she wanted to slam the door shut and pretend he had never come. She had an awful feeling he'd brought terrible news about Ken. She'd known something had happened to him from the moment she'd broken Mama's crystal bud vase.

Mrs. Henley was just coming up the front steps, trudging heavily in her boots and her shabby fur coat with its frayed cuffs where the leather was beginning to show. She saw what Yuki held in her hand.

"It's not bad news is it, Yuki?" she asked.

"I . . . I don't know."

"Is your mama home?"

Yuki shook her head. "She's gone to the market."

Mrs. Henley's face was red from the wind and her breath came in short gasps that left wisps of steam in the brittle, cold air.

Yuki was surprised by the gentleness in her voice. "Don't fret now, my dear," she said softly. "Do you want me to open it for you?"

Yuki nodded. Her throat was tight and dry, and her heart felt as though it might explode. She couldn't talk and she could scarcely think. She was glad to hand the envelope to Mrs. Henley, as though by giving it to her she could be rid of the awful news inside.

Mrs. Henley pulled off her damp gloves and ripped open the envelope. And then she smiled. "Why, Yuki, it's all right," she said brightly. "Your brother's only been wounded. He's been evacuated to a hospital, but he's all right. Maybe he'll even be sent home soon."

Then for the first time she gave Yuki a warm, loving hug, and Yuki hugged her back.

It was funny how the telegram about Ken made them all so happy. Here poor Ken was lying in some hospital with shrapnel wounds in his leg, but Mama and Papa and Yuki were overjoyed because Ken hadn't been killed.

"It's all right now, Mama," Papa said over and over again. "Ken is alive."

And Mama couldn't stop crying because she was so relieved. None of them had dared speak aloud what each feared, but Yuki knew she wasn't the only one who had feared the worst.

"Mrs. Henley said maybe he'd get sent home soon," Yuki said hopefully.

"Oh, I do hope so," Mama answered. "I can't believe he's really all right until I see him with my own eyes." Then she said something else.

"You know, good things often happen in threes. Maybe two more nice things will happen before long."

As usual, Mama was right. A few weeks later, Papa heard that the army had revoked the exclusion order against the Japanese on the West Coast.

Yuki had never seen him so excited in a long time.

"Do you know what that means?" he asked, pacing back and forth in the living room because he couldn't sit still.

"It means we can go back to California now if we want to. It means we can go home to Berkeley. The army can't keep us out any more."

Yuki leaped from her chair and hung on Papa's neck as she used to do when she was little.

"Can we go home then, Papa? Can we go back to Berkeley?"

"I don't see why not," Papa answered quickly. "I'm sure I can find a sponsor there to vouch for me."

"But where will we live?" Mama wondered. "Our old house is rented now to someone else."

"We'll find something," Papa assured her. "Don't worry. We'll find a way." And he went straight to the desk and began writing some letters.

It was a while before the third good thing happened, but it finally did. The Reverend Wada wrote to Papa that he'd gotten permission to leave Camp Topaz and was going back to their Japanese church in Berkeley.

"My wife and I will open our church again and turn it into a hostel so the returning Japanese will have a place to stay until they can find proper housing," he wrote. "Won't you and your family join us as soon as possible and help us open up our church once more? I will secure a sponsor for you, Mr. Sakane, and do whatever is necessary to facilitate your return."

Now they had a place to go and California could no longer keep them out.

"Start packing, Mama," Papa said as soon as he read the Reverend Wada's letter. "We're going home."

Following My Dreams

by *Yoshiko Uchida*

Mother, Yoshiko (age ten), Father,
Grandmother, older sister Keiko

When I was growing up in Berkeley, California, the world was a very different place. I asked such questions as, "Can we swim in your pool even if we're Japanese Americans?" or, "Will the neighbors be angry if we move in next door?" Before going to a beauty parlor, I would call to ask if they cut Japanese hair, and I was often ignored by salesclerks who treated me as though I didn't exist.

A Japanese American family gathers around their table in a World War II internment camp.

My parents created a warm, loving home for my older sister and me, infusing into our lives their own Japanese spirit and values. But I wanted so much to be accepted by white American society that I often rejected my Japaneseness.

One summer when I was ten, I met a white woman whose first words were to compliment me for speaking English so well. I was totally dismayed, for she had seen only my Japanese face and treated me like a foreigner. I realized then that I would always be perceived as being different.

Japanese American children in an internment camp during World War II.

It wasn't until both the world and I had changed drastically that I finally learned to be proud of the Japanese as well as the American part of me. By then I had survived the World War II internment, when our government uprooted and incarcerated 120,000 Japanese Americans without trial or hearing, not because we had committed a crime, but simply because we looked like the enemy.

I wanted young Japanese Americans to be proud of the courage and strength with which their parents and grandparents survived this ordeal. I also wanted all young Americans to know of this tragedy so such an uprooting would never happen again. And so I wrote *Journey to Topaz* and its sequel *Journey Home*.

In these books, Yuki and her family endure much of what my own family did, although the sequel is not our story. Yuki feels the same despair I did when I was sent to a concentration camp. She also has the same longing for home and realizes, as I eventually did, that home is wherever those we love are gathered together.

My parents taught me much about the importance of family, hard work, loyalty, a sense of purpose and affirmation, and holding onto one's dreams. In *A Jar of Dreams* and its two sequels, I evoke similar beliefs and values in Rinko's family because I think they are still important today.

Although these books are totally fictional, there *is* something of me in Rinko. She, however, learned to feel proud of herself earlier than I did—which is the nice thing about fiction. Events can be telescoped, and one can sometimes create satisfying situations not always possible in real life.

I did not have an Aunt Waka, but my parents and their friends were strong, courageous people who, like Aunt Waka, were proud of their heritage and encouraged me to follow my dreams. They passed on to me their strength and Japanese spirit, and when I finally learned to accept myself for what I was—American *and* Japanese—I became whole and happy, just as Rinko did.

Yoshiko Uchida

Thinking About It

1   Yuki was afraid to open the telegram because she was afraid it had bad news. Talk to Yuki. What is the best thing to do when you are afraid you're going to get bad news?

2   You've now read stories from two of Yoshiko Uchida's books. If you could sit down and have a chat with her, what would you ask her? Why?

3   Continue Yuki's story. What do you think the Sakanes find when they get back to California? What do they do?

Another Book
by Yoshiko Uchida

The Invisible Thread: A Memoir is Yoshiko Uchida's autobiography. The parallels and differences between her life and the story of Yuki are fascinating.

SUMMER HOME

from **My People, the Sioux**
by **Chief Luther Standing Bear**

In the early spring, when we moved away
from our winter quarters, our band of
Indians looked better than any circus
parade. Each family had its place in line.

Nobody was ever in a hurry to get ahead of those in advance—as the white man in his automobile tries to do in this day and age.

In traveling, the ponies carrying the tipi poles of one family went along together. Then came the pony that carried the tipi covering. This was folded in such a way that there was equal weight on each side. Next came the ponies with the bags. The rawhide bags hung on the saddle, one on each side of the pony. On top of these were the round bags, and in the center of these was that portion of the bed made from the branches strung on buckskin. As this was usually decorated, when rolled up it showed a great variety of colors.

The very young babies rode in a travois drawn by a very gentle pony, which the mother of the baby led, riding on her own pony. We bigger boys and girls always rode our own ponies, and we had plenty of fun chasing birds and hunting, until we came to the new camping-ground.

In all this hustle and bustle of moving, getting the children ready, and starting on the road, in spite of the fact that there were several hundred people, there was no confusion, no

rushing hither and thither, no swearing and no "bossing."
Every one knew we were moving camp, and
each did his or her duty without orders.
The entire camp would be on the
road without any noise.

The old men of the tribe
would start out first on foot. They
were always in front, and we depended
on them. They were experienced and knew the lay of the land
perfectly. If the start was made before sunrise, it was beautiful
to see the golden glow of the coming day. Then the old men
sat down to wait for the sunrise, while the rest of us stood
about, holding our horses. One of the men would light the
pipe, and, as the sun came over the horizon, the entire tribe
stood still, as the ceremony to the Great Spirit began. It was
a solemn occasion, as the old man held the bowl of the pipe
in both hands, and pointed the stem toward the sky, then
toward the east, south, west, and north, and lastly, to Mother
Earth. An appeal was made during this ceremony; the men
smoked, after which the pipe was put away. Sometimes there
would be something to eat on these occasions. After this
ceremony was over, somehow we felt safer to go on.

The old men took the lead again, and when they reached a nice grassy place, with plenty of wood and water, they sat down. We then knew they had found a camping-place for the night, and everybody was happy. Every one then got busy locating a place to pitch his tipi. But there was no mad rushing around; we all took our time. Each woman put up her own tipi. Soon the whole camp showed a great circle of tipis, the fires were started, and we were shortly ready to eat. Meantime, the men turned the horses loose and attended to their wants.

Sometimes we would start off again the next morning. Sometimes we remained in one place several days. But as we were on our way to our summer home, in the northern part of Nebraska, and the distance was considerable, we children were anxious to be on the go again.

If there was any dispute about starting, the old men went to their tipi and counseled together. If it was decided to

make a long journey the next day, one of the men would go around and warn every one to get to bed early, so as to be all prepared to start early in the morning. The women would make preparations to carry water along, in case we did not find any on the day's march.

Very early the following morning, we could hear the call of the old man as he passed along by the tipis. He would call out "Co-oco-o!" This meant, "Get up"—and we did.

There was no asking of questions, such as, "What time is it?" "Can I lie a little while longer?" We boys always arose at once, to show that we were young men.

Our journey consumed quite a while. But we stopped when we wanted to and stayed as long as we pleased. There was no great rush. But finally we reached our destination, and  our camp was soon settled. Then a scout was picked to go out for buffalo. When the scout returned, the hunters started out, camp was moved near to the place where the buffalo had been located, so the work would not be so hard on the women by being a great distance from camp. When the fresh meat was brought in, we all had a big feast, and were well pleased and satisfied to go to sleep at the end of another day.

Soon the hot summer days arrived. Perhaps the reader may think we had an awful time in a closed tipi, but not so.

Forked branches were cut from the box-elder tree. While this is a very soft wood, at the fork of a branch it is tough. The branches were cut four or five feet long. Sometimes ash was used, but box elder was better.

The tipi, all around, was staked down with pins. The women would pull all these pins out on hot summer days, which left the tipi loose around the bottom. The forked ends of the box-elder branches were then placed through the holes around the edge of the tipi, which elevated the edge some little distance, quite like an open umbrella. This not only increased the size of the tipi, but made the amount of shade greater. When the tipis were kept nice and clean, it was very pleasant to stroll through a great camp when all the tipi bottoms were raised.

During the heated portion of the day, our parents all sat around in the shade, the women making moccasins, leggings, and other wearing apparel, while the men were engaged in making rawhide ropes for their horses and saddles. Some made hunting arrows, while others made shields and warbonnets. All this sort of work was done while the inmates of the camp were resting.

We children ran around and played, having all the fun we could. In the cool of the evening, after the meal was over, all the big people sat outside, leaning against the tipis. Sometimes there would be foot races or pony races, or a ball game. There was plenty we could do for entertainment. Perhaps two or three of the young men who had been on the war-path would dress up in their best clothes, fixing up their best horses with Indian perfume, and tie eagle feathers to the animals' tails and on their own foreheads. When they were "all set" to "show off," they would parade around the camp in front of each tipi—especially where there were pretty girls.

We smaller children sat around and watched them. I recall how I wished that I was big enough so I could ride a perfumed horse, all fixed up, and go to see a pretty girl. But I knew that was impossible until I had been on the war-path, and I was too young for that. Before we could turn our thoughts toward such things, we must first know how to fish, kill game and skin it; how to butcher and bring the meat home; how to handle our horses properly; and be able to go on the war-path.

When the shades of night fell, we went to sleep, unless our parents decided to have a game of night ball. If they did, then we little folks tried to remain awake to watch the fun. We were never told that we must "go to bed," because we never objected or cried about getting up in the morning. When we grew tired of playing, we went to our nearest relatives and stayed at their tipi for the night, and next morning went home.

When a thunderstorm threatened, every one ran to his tipi. All the forked branches were pulled out, and the sides of the tipi were lowered. If a high wind accompanied the storm, the women, boys, and girls were all hustling, pounding the stakes into place with stone hammers. Then the long branches from the box-elder tree were carried inside the tipi to be used as braces for the poles, which kept them from breaking in. After the storm had passed, how fresh and cool all the earth seemed!

Such was the life I lived. We had everything provided for us by the Great Spirit above. Is it any wonder that we grew fat with contentment and happiness?

THINKING ABOUT IT

>1<

Luther Standing Bear seems to have happy memories as he writes about his childhood. When you are fifty years old, what are some happy times you will remember about your childhood?

>2<

Close your eyes. What peaceful scene from this selection can you see in your mind's eye? What does the selection tell you about it, and what do you add?

>3<

If Luther Standing Bear could give you some ideas on making your life better, what would he tell you?

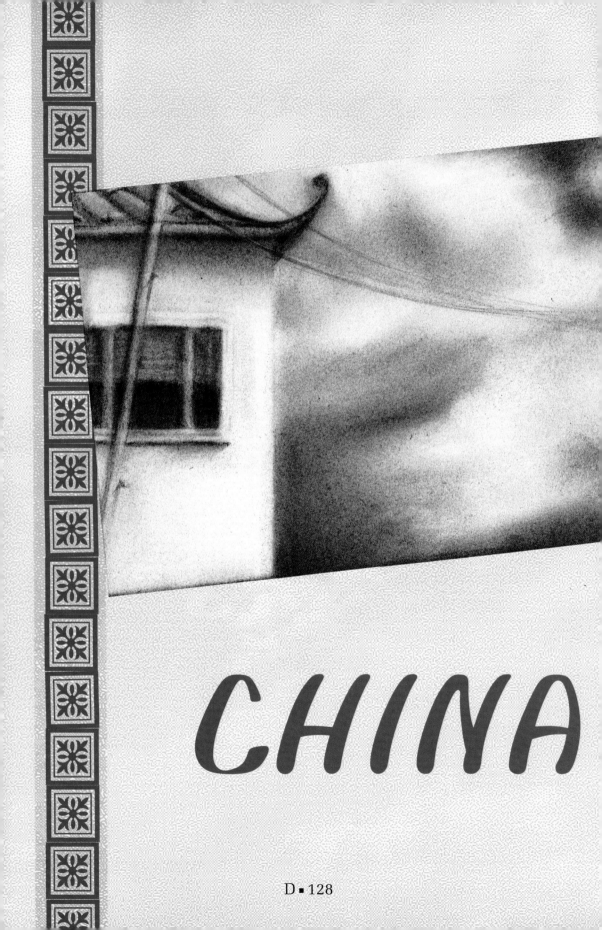

CHINA

TOWN

from
*The
Lost
Garden*

by
Laurence
Yep

When Laurence Yep was growing up in the 1940s and 1950s, he and his family lived in the Pearl Apartments in an integrated neighborhood in San Francisco. However, most Chinese Americans, including some of Laurence Yep's relatives, lived in the neighborhood known as Chinatown.

If Uncle Francis and other members of our family left Chinatown to explore America, my experience was the reverse because I was always going into Chinatown to explore the streets and perhaps find the key to the pieces of the puzzle. But the search only seemed to increase the number of pieces.

When I was a boy, Chinatown was much more like a small town than it is now. It was small not only in terms of population but in physical area as well. Its boundaries were pretty well set by Pacific Avenue on the north next to the Italian neighborhood of North Beach, Kearny Street on the east, Sacramento Street on the south, and Stockton Street on the west—an area only of a few city blocks.

There is a stereotype that the Chinese lived in Chinatown because they wanted to. The fact was that before the fair housing laws they often had no choice.

For years there was a little cottage on an ivy-covered hill in the southwest corner of

Chinatown just above the Stockton tunnel. There was—and still is—very little plant life in Chinatown, so the only color green I saw was the paint on my school. The kind of green that is alive—lawns, bushes, and trees—was something I had to leave China-town to see, except for that ivy-covered slope. On windy days, the ivy itself would stir and move like a living sea; and overlook-ing the ivy was a cottage that was charm itself. However, as much as I admired the house—on occasion I was disloyal enough to the Pearl Apartments to want to live in it—I knew it wasn't for us. My Auntie Mary had once tried to rent it and had been re-fused because she was Chinese.

Out of some forty-five or so students in my class, I was one of the few who lived out-side of Chinatown. Now, thanks to the fair housing laws that were passed in the 1960s, almost none of my former classmates live there; and Chinatown itself has spilled out of its traditional boundaries.

When I was a boy, though, we could see the results of white money and power on three sides of us. To the east we could stare up at the high-rise office buildings of the business district; and to the west, up the steep streets, were the fancy hotels of Nob Hill. Southward lay downtown and the fancy department stores.

Grant Avenue led directly to downtown; but for years I always thought of the Stockton tunnel as the symbolic end to Chinatown. When it had been cut right through a hill,

We could see the fancy hotels on Nob Hill.

my father and his young friends had held
foot races through it after midnight, hooting
and hollering so that the echoes seemed to
be the cheers of a huge crowd. The rich
white world began just on the other side
of the tunnel.

There were also invisible barriers that separated the wealthy whites from the Chinese
who cleaned their apartments or waited on
their tables. The Chinese could see and even
touch the good life; but they could not join in.

One of my classmates, Harold, had a
paper route on Nob Hill. I still find it hard to
believe that, up hills that angled some forty
degrees or so, he carried a kind of poncho

loaded with papers in front and back. But he did that every afternoon. Once I went along with him; and I followed him into one of the fanciest hotels on Nob Hill, past the elaborately uniformed doorman, over the plush carpets, under the ornate chandeliers, and around in back, down concrete hallways as bleak as the ones in the Chinatown housing projects that were painted a cheap, gaudy yellow—a shade which my friend referred to as "landlord yellow." Harold would deliver the afternoon newspapers to the laundrymen and other workers. And with my friend that day, I wandered all around the roots of that palatial dream of wealth.

When the poncho was flat, my friend and I returned to his tenement apartment where there was only one toilet to a floor; and the toilet lacked both a door and toilet paper. When you went, you brought in your own toilet paper. Nothing could be done about the door except changing your attitude about privacy.

Many of my schoolmates lived in the Chinatown projects; and I wasn't sure if life was any better in them than life in the projects near our store. Another newspaper carrier named Paul lived there. As the oldest boy, Paul was expected to look after his younger brothers and sisters while his parents worked—a common practice among many Chinese families. However, as a result, Paul had failed to develop many social skills, let alone improve his English. I remember the nun sending him out on an errand and then

asking the rest of the class to act as his special friend—which was easy for her to say because she was an adult.

As far as I knew, he hung around with his own group in the projects rather than with anyone from school. His group, though, must have been pretty rough because one of them threw a knife that "accidentally" hit Paul in the eye. Fortunately, there was a charity that arranged an operation; and he was given a new eye from someone who had recently died.

We never knew the identity of the donor; but Paul amused himself by claiming it was a rich white. First, he would clap a hand over his new eye and roll his remaining Chinese eye around. Then he would put his hand over his old one and gaze around elaborately with his new American eye. And then he would announce to us that the world looked just the same whether it was a Chinese eye or an American one.

Paul had shot up early and was a giant compared to the rest of us. When he ran, he looked like an ostrich with arms. He would kick out his legs explosively while his arms flailed the air, so it was hard not to laugh; but we didn't because he was also immensely strong.

The playground at St. Mary's was only a concrete basketball court below. Up above, there was a kind of patio between the convent and the school where the younger children could play. However, the nuns were so worried about our knocking one another down that they forbade us to run during recess. About the only thing we could play under those conditions was a kind of slow-motion tag.

At noon, we could go across the street to the Chinese Playground—the playground where my father had once been the director. In those days, it consisted of levels. The first level near the alley that became known as Hang Ah Alley was a volleyball and a tennis court. Down the steps was the next level with a sandbox (which was usually full of fleas), a small director's building, a Ping-Pong table, an area covered by tan bark that housed a slide, a set of bars, and a set of swings and other simple equipment. The level next to the Chinese Baptist church was the basketball court.*

We had Physical Education once a week there. The playground director taught the boys, and I suppose the nun handled the girls. Sometimes it was calisthenics, other times it was baseball played with a tennis ball on the tennis court. There was no pitcher. Rather, the "batter" threw up the ball and hit it with his fist. Because of his size and added arm strength from his own paper route, Paul could hit a home run almost every time, sending the tennis ball flying over the high wire-mesh fence.

However, my experience was frequently the reverse. Because the present director

*Years later, as part of a set of improvements, the city built an elaborate jungle gym in the playground, which upset a number of the older Chinese. "What do they think our children are? Monkeys?"

knew that my father had once been the director of the playground, he was always urging
me on to one disaster after another.

The worst happened when he wasn't present though. In third grade, we had a very
sweet nun, Sister Bridget, who used to play
kickball with us. Kickball was like baseball
except that the pitcher bowled a ball the
size of a basketball over the ground and the
"batter" kicked it. One time someone kicked
a ball so that it rolled foul. Retrieving it, I
threw it to Sister; but as fate would have it,
she had turned her head right at that moment
to look at something else. I wound up hitting
her in the head; and though there was no
physical harm, I broke her glasses. Even
though my parents paid for replacements,

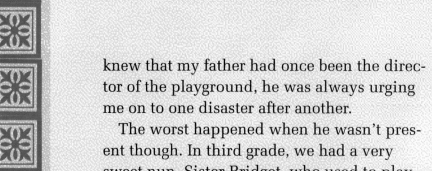

I broke Sister Bridget's glasses.

I was hopeless at catching a pass.

the rest of my class treated me as if I were taboo for striking a nun. I learned what it meant to be shunned and to be invisible.

The experience also reinforced my belief that I was terrible at sports. Despite all the practice and coaching from my father, I was hopeless when it came to catching any ball in any shape or size. Nor could I dribble a basketball, even though my father sometimes kept me practicing in the little courtyard until it was almost too dark to see.

The only sport that I was remotely good at was football. Having worked and lifted crates in the store made me fairly strong. As a result, I was a good lineman at blocking and rushing—like my hero, Leo

Nomellini. However, I was still hopeless at catching a pass. I still remember one game where I dropped three touchdown passes in a row. I was so bad that our opponents stopped covering me. Our quarterback, unable to resist a wide-open target, persisted in throwing to me—and I dropped yet a fourth pass that could have been a touchdown.

The fact that my whole family was athletic only added to my disgrace. My father had played both basketball and football. My mother had also played basketball as well as being a track star, winning gold medals at the Chinese Olympics—a track event held for Chinese Americans. My brother was also excellent at basketball as well as bowling. Even worse, my father had coached championship teams when he had been a director at Chinese Playground—the very site of most of my failures. I often felt as if I were a major disappointment to my family.

Moreover, my lack of Chinese made me an outsider in Chinatown—sometimes even among my friends. Since it was a Catholic school taught by nuns, my friends would always tell dirty jokes in Chinese so the nuns wouldn't understand. However, neither did I, so I missed out on a good deal of humor when I was a boy. What Chinese I did pick up was the Chinese that got spoken in the playground—mostly insults and vulgar names.

There were times even with a good friend like Harold when I felt different. Though Harold and I would go see American war movies, he could also open up a closet and show me the exotic Chinese weapons his father, a gardener, would fashion in his spare time, and I could sense a gulf between my experience and that of Harold's. It was as if we belonged to two different worlds.

Even my friends' games and entertainments in Chinatown could sometimes take their own different spin. They weren't quite like the games I saw American boys playing on television or read about in Homer Price. Handball was played with the all-purpose tennis ball against a brick wall in the courtyard.

Nor do I remember anyone ever drawing a circle with chalk and shooting marbles in the American way. Instead, someone

I missed a lot not knowing Chinese.

would set up marbles on one side of the basketball court at St. Mary's and invite the others to try to hit them. If they did, they got the marbles. If they didn't, the boy would quickly snatch up their shooters. The ideal spot, of course, was where irregularities in the paving created bumps or dips to protect the owner's marbles. At times, one edge of the courtyard would resemble a bazaar with different boys trying to entice shooters to try their particular setup with various shouted jingles.

Other times, they would set up baseball or football cards. Trading cards weren't meant to be collectors' items but were used like marbles. In the case of cards, the shooter would send a card flying with a flick of the wrist. Mint cards did not always fly the truest; and certain cards with the right bends and folds became deadly treasures.

But that sense of being different became sharpest the time I was asked to sing. Our school had a quartet that they sent around to build goodwill. The two girls and two boys dressed up in outfits that were meant to be Chinese: the girls in colored silk pajamas and headdresses with pom-poms, the boys in robes with black vests and caps topped by red knobs.

However, one day in December, one of the boys took sick so the nuns chose me to take his place. Musical ability was not a consideration; the fit of the costume was the important thing. We were brought to sing before a group of elderly people. I can remember following a cowboy with an accordion and a cowgirl with a short, spangled skirt who sang Christmas carols with a country twang.

Then we were ushered out on the small stage and I could look out at the sea of elderly faces. I think they were quite charmed with the costumed Chinese children. Opening their mouths, the others began to sing in Chinese. Now during all this, no one had bothered to find out if I could sing, let alone sing in Chinese. I recognized the tune as "Silent Night" but the words were all in Chinese. I tried to fake it but I was always one note and one pretend-syllable behind the others. Then they

I was always one note behind.

swung into "It Came Upon a Midnight
Clear." This time they sang in English so I
tried to sing along and ranged all over the
musical scale except the notes I was supposed to be singing. Finally, one of the
girls elbowed me in the ribs and from the
side of her mouth, she whispered fiercely,
"Just mouth the words."

Up until then I had enjoyed putting on
costumes and even had a variety of hats,
including cowboy and Robin Hood outfits
as well as a French Foreign Legion hat and
a Roman helmet; but the experience cured
me of wanting to dress up and be something else. How could I pretend to be
somebody else when I didn't even know
who *I* was?

In trying to find solutions, I had created
more pieces to the puzzle: the athlete's son
who was not an athlete, the boy who got
"A's" in Chinese school without learning
Chinese, the boy who could sing neither
in key nor in Chinese with everyone else.

PULLING THE THEME TOGETHER

BELONGING

1

"I failed!"
"I didn't belong!"
Did Laurence Yep really feel that way? What did you learn about what Yep the author is really like?

2

You go to Luther Standing Bear and Laurence Yep and ask them for advice on how to write an interesting autobiography. What do they tell you?

3

You go to each of the main characters or people in the selections you read in *Journey Home* and ask, "Where do you belong? Where are your roots? Where do you call 'home'?" What does each one tell you? Do their answers have anything in common?

BOOKS TO ENJOY

The Man in the Ceiling

by Jules Feiffer
HarperCollins, 1993

Jimmy wants to be a cartoonist. His parents think he's wasting his time. When Charley Beemer, the greatest preteen athlete in the history of Montclair, New Jersey, wants to create cartoons with Jimmy, Jimmy doesn't think life can get any better.

Is Anybody There?

by Eve Bunting
Harper, 1990

Is someone unknown living in the house? Learning the identity of an uninvited guest produces surprising results for Marcus.

Homesick: My Own Story

by Jean Fritz
Putnam, 1982

Jean Fritz's autobiography about growing up in China is filled with vivid descriptions and wonderful anecdotes. Is it possible for a girl to long for her home in America and yet, at the same time, love China so much?

M. C. Higgins, the Great

by Virginia Hamilton
Macmillan, 1974

M. C. Higgins longs to escape from his home next to a smelly spoil heap. Encounters with two strangers may teach him that happiness will not be found by fleeing his home in the hills.

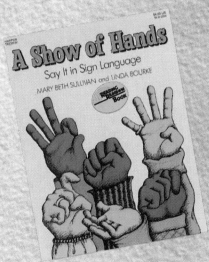

The Happiest Ending

by Yoshiko Uchida
Atheneum, 1985

In the last book of the "Rinko" trilogy, Rinko learns that a neighbor's daughter is coming from Japan to marry a stranger twice her age. Can Rinko block the arrangements in time?

An Actor's Life for Me

by Lillian Gish
Viking, 1987

In this autobiography, Lillian Gish reminisces about her childhood as a stage actress—from the thrill of being on stage to the pain of being separated from her family.

A Show of Hands: Say It in Sign Language

by Mary Beth Sullivan and Linda Bourke
Lippincott, 1980

Prepare to "talk" with your hands! Learn how people communicate with their hands every day and how deaf and hearing-impaired people use sign language to communicate.

LITERARY TERMS

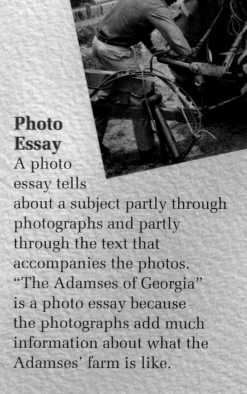

Autobiography

An autobiography is the story of a real person's life written by that person. In "Chinatown," Laurence Yep describes his experiences growing up in San Francisco. In the autobiography, Yep tells you things that made him feel he was not comfortable with his Chinese heritage.

Mood

The mood of a piece of writing is the feeling it creates in you as you read. The mood may be sad, as in "Living with Strangers." In "Apple Is My Sign," a mood of uncertainty exists as Harry tries to get used to his new life in a boarding school.

Photo Essay

A photo essay tells about a subject partly through photographs and partly through the text that accompanies the photos. "The Adamses of Georgia" is a photo essay because the photographs add much information about what the Adamses' farm is like.

Point of View

The point of view is the person an author chooses to tell the story. In "The Circuit," the author, Francisco Jiménez, uses the first-person point of view, as if Panchito were telling the story and calling himself "I." "Apple Is My Sign" is told in the third person. The storyteller is not one of the characters but is a narrator who is watching the scene and using "he," "she," and "they" to refer to the people as the story is told.

Setting

The setting is the time and place in which a story happens. The setting may be very important to the story. "The Circuit" could not take place anywhere except in farming country where migrant workers are needed. "Apple Is My Sign" has to take place in a boarding school in 1899. "Living with Strangers" must take place during World War II.

Tone

Tone is the author's attitude toward the subject of an article or story. The tone may be positive and upbeat, as it is in "Summer Home." The move to the summer home is shown as exciting—something to look forward to. By contrast, the tone in "Living with Strangers" is sad and fearful. Yuki and her family worry about what may happen to them.

GLOSSARY

brocade

caricature of
Abraham Lincoln

Vocabulary from your selections

ag ri cul ture (ag′rə kul′chər), science or
art of cultivating the soil, including
producing crops and raising livestock;
farming. *n.*

ar til ler y (är til′ər ē), mounted guns;
cannon. *n.*

berth (bėrth), **1** a ship's place at a wharf.
2 place for a ship to anchor
conveniently or safely. **3** provide with a
berth; have a berth. 1,2 *n.*, 3 *v.*

bro cade (brō kād′), an expensive cloth
woven with raised designs on it, used
for clothing or upholstery: *silk brocade,
velvet brocade. n.*

car i ca ture (kar′ə kə chùr), picture,
cartoon, or description that exaggerates
the features or mannerisms of a person
or the defects of a thing. *n.*

cer e mo ny (ser′ə mō′nē), a special act
or set of acts to be done on special
occasions such as weddings, funerals,
graduations, or holidays: *The
graduation ceremony was held in the
gymnasium. n., pl.* **cer e mo nies.**

cir cuit (sėr′kit), route over which a
person or group makes repeated
journeys at certain times: *Some judges
make a circuit, stopping at certain
towns along the way to hold court. n.*

com mem o rate (kə mem′ə rat′),
preserve or honor the memory of: *a
stamp commemorating the landing of
the Pilgrims. v.,* **com mem o rat ed,
com mem o rat ing.**

com mem o ra tion (kə mem′ə rā′shən),
1 act of commemorating. **2** service or
celebration in memory of some person
or event. *n.*

con sume (kən süm′), use up; spend: *A student consumes much time in studying. I consumed almost all the money I earned last summer. v.,* **con sumed, con sum ing.**

con tent ment (kən tent′mənt), a being satisfied or pleased; ease of mind. *n.*

co-op (kō′op), INFORMAL. cooperative. *n.*

co op er a tive (kō op′ər ə tiv *or* kō op′ə rā′tiv), **1** wanting or willing to work together with others: *The pupils were helpful and cooperative.* **2** union of farmers for buying and selling their produce at the best price. 1 *adj.,* 2 *n.*

crip ple (krip′əl), person or animal that cannot use an arm or leg properly because of injury or deformity; lame person or animal. *n.*

e lat ed (i lā′tid), in high spirits; joyful: *We are elated about good news. adj.*

e vac u ate (i vak′yü āt), withdraw; remove: *Efforts were made to evacuate all civilians from the war zone. v.,* **e vac u at ed, e vac u at ing.**

ex ot ic (eg zot′ik), foreign; strange; not native: *We saw many exotic plants at the flower show. adj.*

gal va nize (gal′və nīz), cover (iron or steel) with a thin coating of zinc to prevent rust. *v.,* **gal va nized, gal va- niz ing.** —**gal′va nized,** *adj.*

graze (grāz), feed on growing grass: *Cattle were grazing in the field. v.,* **grazed, graz ing.**

im mi gra tion (im′ə grā′shən), a coming into a country or region to live there: *There has been immigration to America from many countries. n.*

in car ce rate (in kär′sə rāt′), put in prison. *v.,* **in car ce rat ed, in car ce rat ing.**

in tern (in tėrn′), confine within a country or place; force to stay in a certain place, especially during wartime. *v.*

in tern ment (in tėrn′mənt), an interning or a being interned; confinement within a country or place. *n.*

ja lop y (jə lop′ē), INFORMAL. an old automobile in bad condition. *n., pl.* **ja lop ies.**

a	hat	oi	oil
ā	age	ou	out
ä	far	u	cup
e	let	ù	put
ē	equal	ü	rule
ėr	term		
i	it	ch	child
ī	ice	ng	long
o	hot	sh	she
ō	open	th	thin
ô	order	ᴛʜ	then
		zh	measure

ə = {
a in about
e in taken
i in pencil
o in lemon
u in circus
}

exotic—an **exotic** fish

kimono

ki mo no (kə mō′nə), a loose outer garment held in place by a sash, worn by Japanese men and women. *n.*, *pl.* **ki mo nos.**

o men (ō′mən), sign of what is to happen; object or event that is believed to mean good or bad fortune: *Spilling salt is said to be an omen of bad luck. n.*

pa role (pə rōl′), conditional release from prison or jail before the full term is served. *n.*

phase (fāz), carry out or adjust by stages: *phase an army's withdrawal. v.* **phase out,** discontinue or eliminate as a phase or by phases.

proc tor (prok′tər), officer in a university or school who keeps good order. *n.*

proj ect (proj′ekt), **1** a plan; scheme: *a project for slum clearance.* **2** a special assignment planned and carried out by a student, a group of students, or an entire class. **3** group of apartment buildings built and run as a unit, especially with government support. *n.*

re voke (ri vōk′), take back; repeal; cancel; withdraw: *revoke a driver's license. v.,* **re voked, re vok ing.**

sa vor (sā′vər), **1** a taste or smell; flavor: *The soup has a savor of onion.* **2** enjoy the taste or smell of; enjoy very much: *He savored the soup.* **1** *n.,* **2** *v.*

share crop per (sher′krop′ər *or* shar′krop′ər), person who farms land for the owner in return for part of the crops. *n.*

shrap nel (shrap′nəl), **1** shell filled with fragments of metal and powder, set to explode in midair and scatter the fragments over a wide area. **2** metal fragments of an exploding shell. *n.*

shun (shun), keep away from; avoid: *She shuns housework. v.,* **shunned, shun ning.**

sol emn (sol′əm), **1** serious; grave; earnest: *to speak in a solemn voice. I gave my solemn promise to do better.* **2** done with form and ceremony: *a solemn procession.* **3** connected with religion; sacred. *adj.*

ster e o type (ster′ē ə tīp′ *or* stir′ē ə tīp′), a fixed form, character, image, etc.; conventional type. Long John Silver, in Stevenson's *Treasure Island,* is the stereotype of a pirate. *n.*

syn thet ic (sin thet′ik), made artificially by forming a compound through chemical reactions. Nylon is a synthetic fiber. Many kinds of fabrics, furs, dyes, rubbers, and drugs are synthetic products. *adj.*

te di ous (tē′dē əs *or* tē′jəs), long and tiring: *A boring talk is tedious. adj.*

ten e ment (ten′ə mənt), a building, especially in a poor section of a city, divided into sets of rooms occupied by separate families. *n.*

tex tile (tek′stəl *or* tek′stīl), **1** a woven fabric; cloth: *Beautiful textiles are sold in Paris.* **2** material that can be woven. **3** of the making, selling, etc., of textiles: *the textile industry.* 1,2 *n.,* 3 *adj.*

tra vois (trə voi′), vehicle without wheels used by Great Plains Indians, consisting of two shafts or poles joined by a platform or net for holding the load. *n., pl.* **tra vois.**

a	hat	oi	oil
ā	age	ou	out
ä	far	u	cup
e	let	ù	put
ē	equal	ü	rule
ėr	term		
i	it	ch	child
ī	ice	ng	long
o	hot	sh	she
ō	open	th	thin
ô	order	₮H	then
		zh	measure

ə = {
a in about
e in taken
i in pencil
o in lemon
u in circus
}

travois

ACKNOWLEDGMENTS

Text

Page 7: "Apple Is My Sign" from *Apple Is My Sign* by Mary Riskind. Copyright © 1981 by Mary Riskind. Reprinted by permission of Houghton Mifflin Company.

Page 34: "In a Deaf World" by Mary Riskind. Copyright © 1991 by Mary Riskind.

Page 43: "The Circuit" by Francisco Jiménez from *The Arizona Quarterly,* Autumn 1973. Reprinted by permission of the author.

Page 58: "Lyle" from *Bronzeville Boys and Girls* by Gwendolyn Brooks. Copyright © 1956 by Gwendolyn Brooks Blakely. Reprinted by permission of HarperCollins *Publishers.*

Page 60: "The Way" from *Collected Poems by Edwin Muir.* Copyright © 1960 by Willa Muir. Reprinted by permission of Oxford University Press, Inc., and Faber and Faber Limited.

Page 62: "The Adamses of Georgia" from *The American Family Farm: A Photo Essay* by George Ancona, text by Joan Anderson. Text copyright © 1989 by Joan Anderson. Reprinted by permission of Harcourt Brace Jovanovich, Inc.

Page 79: "Waka's Gift" reprinted with permission of Margaret K. McElderry Books, an imprint of Macmillan Publishing Company, from *A Jar of Dreams* by Yoshiko Uchida. Copyright © 1981 by Yoshiko Uchida.

Page 97: "Living with Strangers" reprinted with permission of Margaret K. McElderry Books, an imprint of Macmillan Publishing Company, from *Journey Home* by Yoshiko Uchida. Copyright © 1978 by Yoshiko Uchida.

Page 112: "Following My Dreams" by Yoshiko Uchida. Copyright © 1991 by Yoshiko Uchida.

Page 117: "Summer Home," excerpt from *My People, the Sioux* by Luther Standing Bear. Copyright © 1928 by Luther Standing Bear. Reprinted by permission of Geoffrey Standing Bear.

Page 129: "Chinatown" from the book *The Lost Garden* by Laurence Yep. Copyright © 1991 by Laurence Yep. Used by permission of the publisher, Julian Messner/A division of Silver Burdett Press, Inc., Simon & Schuster, Englewood Cliffs, NJ.

Artists

Illustrations owned and copyrighted by the illustrator.

Cover: Teresa Fasolino

Pages 1–4: Teresa Fasolino

Pages 6, 26, 34: John Craig

Pages 42–57, 143: José Ortega

Pages 78–111, 143: Jeff Smith

Pages 83, 91: John Gampert

Pages 117–126,143: Sioux art

Pages 128–142: Scott Hunt

Photographs

Page 34: Courtesy of Mary Riskind

Pages 62-77,143: George Ancona

Pages 74-75: Art Wolfer/All Star

Page 112: Courtesy of Yoshiko Uchida

Page 113(T): FTG International

Page 113(B): FTG International

Pages 116, 121: Courtesy of Geoffrey Standing Bear

Page 149: A. Visage/Gamma-Liaison

Page 151: James Jerome Hill Reference Library, St. Paul, MN

Unless otherwise acknowledged, all photographs are the property of Scott-Foresman.

Glossary

The contents of the Glossary entries in this book have been adapted from *Scott, Foresman Intermediate Dictionary,* Copyright © 1988 by Scott, Foresman and Company, and *Scott, Foresman Advanced Dictionary,* Copyright © 1988 by Scott, Foresman and Company.